# FREE $TUFF FOR COOKS

## FREE $TUFF FOR COOKS

### The Free Stuff Editors

*Director:* Bruce Lansky
*Editor:* Tom Grady
*Executive Editor:* Kathe Grooms
*Editorial Assistant:* Kathleen Crepeau

*Art Director:* Terry Dugan
*Asst. Art Director:* Marcia Conley
*Illustrator:* Sandra Hawk

---

### OUR PLEDGE

We have selected the best of all offers available. The suppliers have promised, in writing, to honor single copy requests through 1981 — and beyond, as long as supplies last. We will monitor the suppliers and keep the book updated and accurate. We're dedicated to making this a book that really works.

## Meadowbrook Press
Wayzata, Minnesota 55391

Library of Congress Cataloging in Publication Data

Free Stuff for Cooks

Includes index.
1. Cookery — Catalogs.          2. Free material.
TX652.F695          641.5'0216          80-15462
ISBN 0-915658-23-2

**First Printing May 1980**

Printed in the United States of America
ISBN 0-915658-23-2
Copyright © 1980 by Meadowbrook Press

# CONTENTS

## About This Book

*Free Stuff for Cooks* is a collection of the best materials available through the mail to cooks and foodlovers. In it you'll find descriptions of all kinds of recipe booklets, buying and nutrition guides, catalogs, and product samples that various organizations have agreed to send to readers who write them. And as a bonus, on most pages you'll find sample recipes or tips reprinted from the materials described there.

Most of the over 250 items in *Free Stuff for Cooks* are available for the price of a postcard. However, because of the high cost of return postage, a number of suppliers ask for a self-addressed, stamped envelope, and some require postage and handling costs that range from 10¢ to $1.00. Still, for very little cost, you can build an extensive home library of cooking and nutrition information.

To put this book together, we did more than simply collect whatever offers we could find in newspapers and magazines and on the labels of cans and the backs of boxes. In every case we've gone right to the source. We have contacted each supplier, inspected and evaluated all items, and secured not only the supplier's permission to list a particular offer, but a written guarantee that it will be available **through** 1981 and beyond, as long as supplies last.

Though mistakes do happen, we've tried our best to make sure you get what you send for. And we'd like to thank the organizations listed here for their help and cooperation in making this possible.

**Note on government publications:** We've been in close contact with the

1

government agencies whose publications are listed in *Free Stuff for Cooks,* and we have every assurance that these publications will be available through 1981. But because of the vagaries of government budgets and the volume of requests these agencies get, it's possible that some of their publications may be temporarily unavailable at certain times.

# What's in This Book

1.  Directions on how to send for

    - over 101 recipe booklets, pamphlets and cards;

    - over 50 kitchen guides with information on buying, cooking, storing, freezing and canning foods; plus tips on buying cookware;

    - over 25 booklets and pamphlets about nutrition, health, food labels and diets;

    - dozens of catalogs from mail order food and cookware companies and cookbook publishers; and

    - posters, product samples, and food and nutrition newsletters.

2.  Precise descriptions of the contents, format and length of each item. A **foldout** is a single sheet of paper folded up. A **booklet** is a small, staple-bound book. A **pamphlet** is a narrower booklet.

3.  Sample recipes, tips and other information reprinted from the publications described, making *Free Stuff for Cooks* a book that you can use immediately.

4.  An index that will direct you to all the materials on any particular topic you're interested in, like microwave cooking or cooking with wine.

# How to Use This Book

- Please ask for only **one** copy of each item you're interested in.

- Ask for each item by title if one is given. If no title is provided, describe the item briefly. Ask for all government publications by name and number.

- Make each request as brief as possible and always note what you've enclosed in your envelope. For instance, if you want to send for the first item on page 11, merely write:

> Please send me 1 copy of "Game Recipes." I've enclosed 25¢ and a self-addressed stamped envelope.

- Always write your name and address on both the envelope and on the letter you send.

- If the directions say to send a post-card (and many do), please comply with them. Suppliers can answer your requests more promptly if you do, plus it saves you money. (Remember that the post office will no longer deliver a card that's smaller than 3½x5½ inches.)

- If the instructions say to send money, please send the fewest coins possible, and tape them to the letter you send so they won't rip or fall out of your envelope. Please don't send stamps.

- If the suppliers require a self-addressed, stamped envelope, it's very important that you enclose a **9"-long business envelope.** Most of the "free stuff" won't fit in a smaller envelope.

- Be prepared to wait 4 to 8 weeks for your materials to arrive. You could be surprised with a quicker reply, but you may also have to wait a little longer if a particular organization gets a lot of requests in a short period of time.

**Important Note:** the organizations that supply this "free stuff" are under absolutely no obligation to reply to requests that are improperly made (and they can't respond to requests that they can't read). So if you don't send the right amount of money or if you fail to include a 9" self-addressed, stamped envelope, please don't expect a reply.

# RECIPES

5

# RECIPES

## Steakburgers

Fourteen recipes for making a variety of hamburgers using A.1. Steak Sauce. Includes a basic hamburger recipe, plus tips for creating "international" sandwiches, like the Greek burger (with feta cheese and pita bread) or the Swedish burger (using cucumbers, scallions and sour cream).

**Send:** 50⁵.
**To:** A.1. International Steakburgers, P.O. Box 311K, Dallas, TX 75221

## Beef Microwave

A short, informative foldout, called "Cooking Beef in the Microwave," that answers the questions most often asked about microwave cooking. Discusses what cuts of beef cook best in a microwave and how to prevent beef from toughening. Also contains 6 recipes, including one for Chinese Beef with Broccoli.

**Send:** a 9″ self-addressed, stamped envelope.
**To:** Minnesota Beef Council, 2950 Metro Dr., Suite 111, Minneapolis, MN 55420

## Microwave Cooking

A foldout, called "Beef in the Microwave," that supplies the basics of microwave beef cookery, with tips on timing, tenderness, browning and cooking speed. Also includes recipes for main dishes like Beef Steak Strips, Sukiyaki, and Beef Quiche.

**Send:** 10⁵ plus a 9″ self-addressed, stamped envelope.
**To:** Beef in the Microwave, Iowa Beef Industry Council, P.O. Box 451, Ames, IA 50010

## Hamburgers

### Basic A.1. Hamburgers

1½ lbs. ground beef
1½ t salt
¼ C A.1. Steak
    Sauce

In medium bowl, lightly combine all ingredients. Form 6 patties to fit bread shape of your choice. Broil, barbecue or pan fry until cooked as desired. Makes 6.

Reprinted with permission of Heublein.

### Greek Burgers

1 C Feta cheese, rinsed and crumbled
¼ C sliced ripe olives
1 T A.1. Steak Sauce
1 t lemon juice
2 T mayonnaise

6 Basic A.1. Hamburgers, cooked
3 pita (or pocket) bread, cut in half
6 tomato slices
Shredded lettuce

Combine cheese, olives, A.1., lemon juice and mayonnaise. Place hamburgers in pita bread. Spoon topping over hamburgers. Heat in preheated 425°F oven 5 minutes. Garnish with tomato and lettuce. Serves 6.

# RECIPES

## Lamb

A large 246-page cookbook, called "Lamb Around the World," full of information about lamb, tips for cooking it, time and temperature tables, and hundreds of domestic and foreign recipes for stews, casseroles, kabobs, soups, salads, sandwiches and appetizers.

**Send:** $1.00. *7-1-80*
**To:** Lamb Education Center, Dept. MP, B—114, 200 Clayton St., Denver, CO 80206

## Microlamb

"Microlamb" — recipes for 16 lamb dishes that can be prepared in a microwave. Contains ideas for main dishes like Barbecued Rolled Leg of Lamb, East Indian Lamb and Eggplant, and Lamb Stuffed Peppers. Also includes basic microwave tips.

**Send:** 50¢.
**To:** Lamb Education Center, Dept. MP, B—159, 200 Clayton St., Denver, CO 80206

### Autumn Lamb Stew

2 T butter
1½ lbs. diced lamb shoulder
1 medium-sized onion, sliced
½ C chopped celery
1 small clove garlic, crushed
1 medium-sized green pepper, chopped

2 C stock or bouillon
6 small potatoes, pared and quartered
4 small carrots, diced
1 C diced eggplant
1½ t salt
¼ t pepper
¼ C all-purpose flour
½ C water

Melt butter; add lamb and cook over low heat, stirring occasionally, until browned on all sides. Add onion, celery, garlic and green pepper and cook 5 minutes. Add stock or bouillon. Cover and cook 30 minutes. Add potatoes and cook 10 minutes. Add carrots, eggplant, salt and pepper and cook, covered, 10 minutes, or until vegetables are tender. Remove lamb and vegetables. Combine flour and water; blend. Add flour mixture to stock or bouillon mixture; blend. Cook over low heat, stirring constantly until thickened. Add vegetables and lamb to stock or bouillon mixture. Makes 6 servings.

Reprinted with permission of the Lamb Education Center.

## Pork Savings

A 32-page booklet of "Penny Wise Pork Recipes" for the budget-minded. Includes recipes for casseroles like Smoked Pork and Noodle Bake, sandwiches like Pork Barbecues, and main dishes like Pork Balls on Parslied Noodles. *7-1-80*

**Send:** a 9″ self-addressed, stamped envelope.
**To:** Recipes, Missouri Pork Producers Assn., 922 Fourth St., #10B, Boonville, MO 65233

## Pork for Two

A colorful 32-page booklet, called "Pork for Two," that shows you how to prepare pork dishes that are just the right size for one or two persons. Recipes include South Pacific Pork Kabobs and Fruit Glazed Butterfly Chops. Also describes how to use leftovers in special dishes.

**Send:** a 9″ self-addressed, stamped envelope.
**To:** Recipes, Missouri Pork Producers Assn., 922 Fourth St., #10A, Boonville, MO 65233

## Microwave Pork

Thirty-two pages of "Pork Microwave Recipes" in a booklet that explains the basics of cooking roasts, chops, ham, ribs, bacon and sausage in a microwave. Includes recipes for preparing special dishes like Creole Chops and Barbecue Pork Regal.

**Send:** a 7½x5½-inch self-addressed, stamped envelope.
**To:** Recipes, Missouri Pork Producers Assn., 922 Fourth St., #10C, Boonville, MO 65233

### Creole Chops
(in a microwave)

4 pork rib chops (4 oz. each)
1 medium onion, chopped
1 small green pepper, sliced
½ C chopped celery
2 t parsley flakes
1 t salt
½ t pepper
1/8 t garlic powder
1 can (16 oz.) stewed tomatoes
Dash bottled hot pepper sauce

Place pork chops in 13x9x2-inch baking dish. Top with onion, green pepper and celery. Cook, covered with clear plastic wrap, at Medium High for 7 minutes, giving dish half a turn once. Sprinkle chops with parsley, salt, pepper and garlic. Add tomatoes and hot pepper sauce. Cook, covered, at Medium High for 9 minutes or till pork is done, giving dish a half turn once. Makes 4 servings.

Reprinted with permission of the Missouri Pork Producers Assn.

# RECIPES

## Food Machine

An 8-page color brochure that describes the Kenwood Chef, a versatile food preparation machine that grinds, chops, shreds, peels, kneads, purees, grates — it performs up to 55 separate tasks in all. Twelve gourmet recipes illustrate what the machine can do.

**Send:** a postcard.
**To:** Recipe Offer, Thorn Kenwood Inc., 26 Columbia Turnpike, Florham Park, NJ 07932

## Sausages

An assortment of "Sausage Recipes" that describe dozens of ways to use Oscar Mayer's products — bacon, sausage, cold cuts, etc. — in all kinds of meals. Includes ideas for parties, snacks, cookouts, buffets and other occasions.

**Send:** a postcard. 7·1·80
**To:** Consumer Affairs Dept., Oscar Mayer & Co., P.O. Box 7188—FSFC, Madison, WI 53707

### Hot German Potato Salad

1 pkg. (½ lb.) Oscar Mayer Bacon
3 T sugar
2 T instant minced onion
1 T flour
1½ t salt
½ t celery seed
¼ t pepper
½ C water
⅓ C vinegar
2 cans (1 lb. each) sliced potatoes, drained

Cut bacon into 1-inch pieces. Cook in skillet until crisp; remove and drain, reserving 2 tablespoons drippings. Combine sugar, onion, flour and seasonings; stir into drippings. Gradually add water and vinegar. Heat to boiling, stirring constantly. Add potatoes and bacon pieces. Cook slowly, stirring occasionally, 5 minutes, or until heated through. Makes 6 servings.

Reprinted with permission of Oscar Mayer & Co.

10

# RECIPES

## Cooking Game

A foldout full of game recipes, side dishes and tips for accompanying wines. Includes basic instructions for fixing pheasant, quail, dove, woodcock, duck, squirrel and rabbit, plus dishes like "Flamed Grouse" and "Pheasant Dumpling Pie." Domestic meats can be substituted.

**Send:** 25¢ plus a 9″ self-addressed, stamped envelope.
**To:** Game Recipes, P.O. Box 638, Wayzata, MN 55391

## Chicken

A 128-page cookbook, called "The Chicken Cookbook," that features the recipes submitted by state finalists to the annual National Chicken Cooking Contest. Also includes cutting and boning diagrams, pages of helpful tips, general cooking instructions and information on how to enter the contest yourself.

**Send:** $1.00.
**To:** Chicken Cookbook—FS, Dept. NBC, P.O. Box 307, Coventry, CT 06238

## Cooking Contest

An entry blank that tells you how to enter and spells out the rules for the National Chicken Cooking Contest, sponsored each year by the National Broiler Council. Contest costs nothing to enter and has a first prize of $10,000. Includes a sample recipe.

**Send:** a 9″ self-addressed, stamped envelope.
**To:** National Chicken Cooking Contest, c/o National Broiler Council, 1155-15th St., N.W., Suite 614, Washington, DC 20005

### Flamed Grouse

2 grouse (or 1 pheasant or rabbit, or 2 whole chicken breasts)
2 T butter
Salt and pepper to taste
2 oz. brandy
4 green onions, chopped

1 carrot, minced
1 T chopped (or dried) parsley
1 pinch each of thyme, marjoram
2 T flour
1 C chicken bouillon
½ C dry white wine
2 C sliced mushrooms

Disjoint meat and rub with salt and pepper. Brown in butter for 5 minutes. Pour brandy over meat and light it; allow it to burn out. Add onions, carrot, parsley, thyme and marjoram; brown 2 to 3 minutes. Sprinkle flour over all, stir to blend well, and then stir in the bouillon, wine and mushrooms. Cover and simmer 25-30 minutes for grouse, or longer (until tender) for pheasant or rabbit.

**Tip:** Reserve a teaspoonful of brandy when you pour the rest on the meat, let the brandy in the pan warm a moment, and then light the reserved spirits in the spoon. Lower the flaming spoon into the pan and lean back!

Reprinted with permission of Recipes, Inc.

# RECIPES

## Freshwater Fish

A foldout containing recipes for fixing freshwater fish in various ways. Includes "Pan-Fried Trout," "All-Purpose Beer Batter," "Hearty Fish Chowder" and other baking, poaching, grilling and pickling recipes. Also describes how to make your own tartar sauce, white wine sauce and other accompaniments.

**Send:** 25ᶜ plus a 9″ self-addressed, stamped envelope.
**To:** Fish Recipes, P.O. Box 638, Wayzata, MN 55391

## Salmon

An even dozen salmon recipes in a short foldout called "Simply Salmon." Includes ways of using salmon, which is low in fat and high in protein, in a variety of appetizers, chowders, salads, quiches and souffles.

**Send:** a postcard.
**To:** Castle & Cooke Foods, Free Stuff: Simply Salmon, P.O. Box 7758, San Francisco, CA 94119

## Caviar

A small 20-page booklet, "The Caviar Way of Life," that shows you how you can use Romanoff's "affordable" caviars in a variety of ways, including salads like Chilled Shrimp with Caviar Dressing, appetizers like Caviar-Stuffed Mushrooms, and light suppers like Caviar Crepes.

**Send:** 50ᶜ.
**To:** Romanoff Caviar Co., P.O. Box 566, Dept. FS, Teaneck, NJ 07666

### Sesame Salmon Boats

1 can (7 ¾ oz.) Bumble Bee Red Salmon
1 avocado
Crisp salad greens

Lemon juice
¼ C mayonnaise
¼ t dill weed
¼ t garlic salt
2 t toasted sesame seeds

Drain salmon. Remove skin, if desired. Mash bones. Halve avocado; remove seed. Place each half on a salad plate lined with crisp salad greens. Sprinkle with lemon juice. Combine mayonnaise, dill weed, garlic salt and 1 teaspoon sesame seeds. Fold in salmon and mashed bones. Spoon into avocado halves. Sprinkle with remaining sesame seeds to serve. Makes 2 servings.

Reprinted with permission of Castle & Cooke Foods.

# Tuna

A 21-page booklet, "Tuna: As You Like It," that presents a brief history of the tuna canning industry, plus recipes for dozens of tuna dishes, like Curried Tuna, Tuna Romanoff, Tuna Salad with Sauce Pacific, and many other casseroles, salads and appetizers.

**Send:** a postcard.
**To:** Tuna Research Foundation, Suite 603, 1101-17th St., N.W., Washington, DC 20036

# Sardines

A short pamphlet full of "Maine Sardine Recipes." Includes tips for using sardines in salads, snacks, and main dishes, like Stuffed Peppers and Sardine Pizza, and a chart that compares the nutritional value of sardines with that of tuna, salmon and various luncheon meats.

**Send:** a postcard.
**To:** Maine Sardine Council, P.O. Box 337, Brewer, ME 04412

# French Foods

A small foldout, called "Bon Appetit," that describes a half-dozen French dishes that can be made in a blender. Includes recipes for Pate, Quiche, Hollandaise Sauce, and Raspberry Mousse.

**Send:** a 9" self-addressed, stamped envelope.
**To:** Recipes—French, Oster—FS, P.O. Box 17000, Milwaukee, WI 53217

## Quiche Lorraine

4 eggs
1½ C light cream or undiluted evaporated milk
1 T flour
½ t salt
¼ t pepper
¼ t nutmeg
1 medium onion, cut in eighths

1½ C Swiss cheese, cut in 1" cubes
1 lb. pork sausage, crisply fried and crumbled

or

¾ lb. sliced bacon, crisply fried and crumbled
1 9-inch unbaked pie shell

Preheat oven to 375°F. Put eggs, light cream or evaporated milk, flour, salt, pepper and nutmeg into Osterizer blender container, cover and process at Mix (Lo) until well blended. Stop blender and add the onion pieces and Swiss cheese cubes. Cover and process 3 cycles at Grind (Hi).
Sprinkle crumbled sausage into bottom of unbaked pie shell and pour egg mixture into pie shell. Bake for 35-45 minutes or until a knife inserted into center comes out clean. Yield: 1 9" quiche.

Reprinted with permission of Oster.

13

# RECIPES

## Danish Foods

A 10-page handout of "Danish Recipes" that shows you how to cook what the Danes cook. You'll learn how to make Herring Salad, Danish Meat Balls, Boiled Cod, Roast Pork with Cracklin's, Gloegg and a variety of salads, desserts and open-faced sandwiches.

**Send:** a postcard.
**To:** Royal Danish Consulate General, Danish Information Office, 280 Park Ave., New York, NY 10017

## Scandinavian

"Taste Treasures from Scandinavia," a small recipe foldout that describes 9 Scandinavian dishes that can be made in a blender. Includes Danish Appetizer Meat Balls, Cold Fruit Soup, Danish Rum Pudding and Mazarine Torte.

**Send:** a 9" self-addressed, stamped envelope.
**To:** Recipes—Scandinavian, Oster—FS, P.O. Box 17000, Milwaukee, WI 53217

### Tuna Salad — Swedish Style

1 can (7 oz.) tuna, drained
1 can (4½ oz.) shrimp, drained
2 hard-cooked eggs, quartered
½ C mayonnaise
½ lemon, peeled and seeded, cut in pieces
2 ¼" slices onion
3 8" stalks celery, cut in 1" pieces

Break tuna into chunks in a medium bowl. Put shrimp in Osterizer container, cover and chop by turning control to Lo and Off quickly several times. Add to tuna. Chop eggs, one at a time, in same manner and add to tuna and shrimp.

Put mayonnaise and lemon into Osterizer container, cover and process at Lo until lemon is liquified. Stop Osterizer and add onion and celery. Cover and process at Hi only until celery is chopped. Pour over mixture in bowl and toss well. Chill well and serve on a bed of greens garnished with slices of hard-cooked eggs. Yield: 4-6 servings.

Reprinted with permission of Oster.

# Pennsylvania Dutch

A short foldout with recipes "From the Kitchens of the Pennsylvania Dutch" that can be prepared in a blender. Includes dishes like Dutch Slaw, Hot Bacon Dressing and Kartoffel Pfannkuchen (potato pancakes).

**Send:** a 9″ self-addressed, stamped envelope.
**To:** Recipes—Dutch, Oster—FS, P.O. Box 17000, Milwaukee, WI 53217

# Mexican Dishes

A small foldout, called a "Fiesta of Mexican Cookery," that lists the recipes of 10 dishes like Avocado Soup, Corn Bread, Guacamole Dip and Enchiladas. All recipes call for the use of a blender.

**Send:** a 9″ self-addressed, stamped envelope.
**To:** Recipes—Mexican, Oster—FS, P.O. Box 17000, Milwaukee, WI 53217

# Mexican Favorites

Twenty-two pages of recipes (over 30 in all) for Mexican dishes like Gazpacho, Chile Rellenos and Mexican Spareribs. Written in an easy-to-follow form for the modern cook who wants to use modern appliances. Ask for the "Favorite Mexican Foods Cookbook."

**Send:** $1.00.
**To:** Pecos River Spice Co., P.O. Box 680F, New York, NY 10021

## Gazpacho
(Cold Spanish Soup)

1 C tomato juice
1 T wine vinegar
3 T olive oil
¼ t garlic salt
1 med. onion, peeled and quartered (prefer mild tasting purple onion)
4 large very ripe tomatoes, peeled and chopped

1 large cucumber, peeled and chopped
1 green pepper (bell or chili — depending on taste preference) seeded and quartered
Freshly ground black pepper

Place tomato juice, wine vinegar, olive oil, garlic salt and onion in blender. Blend a few seconds on high speed until onion is pulverized.

Add the rest of the ingredients to the blender and blend on a slow speed until a smooth texture is obtained. If preferred, finely chop the remaining ingredients and stir together. Season with a few grinds of black pepper and salt if desired and chill for at least one hour before serving. Serve in small glasses, bowls, or goblets lined with lettuce leaves. Yield: 8 large or 16 small servings.

Reprinted with permission of the Pecos River Spice Co.

# RECIPES

## Irish Mist

Thirty-two pages of recipes featuring Irish Mist, in a booklet called "The Legendary Spirit." Shows you how to make appetizers, main dishes (like Finnegan's Flounder), desserts and a variety of drinks (like Irish Mist Collins).

**Send:** a postcard.
**To:** Consumer Affairs Dept., Heublein Spirits Group, 330 New Park Ave., Hartford, CT 06101

## Cordials

A 50-page booklet, "Endless Enjoyment—Easy Entertaining," with recipes for drinks, main dishes, and desserts made with Arrow cordials, liqueurs and brandies. Booklet is designed so the pages can be separated and added to a recipe card file.

**Send:** a postcard.
**To:** Consumer Affairs Dept., Heublein Spirits Group, 330 New Park Ave., Hartford, CT 06101

## Wine Recipes

A selection of "Wine Recipes" from Widmer's Wine Cellars. Recipes will help you prepare all sorts of meat and fish dishes, appetizers, desserts, sauces and jellies with a little wine.

**Send:** a 9" self-addressed, stamped envelope.
**To:** Marketing Services, Widmer's Wine Cellars, Inc., West Ave., Naples, NY 14512

### Finnegan's Flounder

2 lbs. flounder fillets
1 small onion, chopped
1 t salt
Freshly ground pepper
¾ C apple juice
¼ C Irish Mist
¼ C lemon juice

2 T butter (or margarine)
2 T flour
¼ C heavy cream
¼ C (2 oz.) freshly shredded Parmesan cheese
Finely minced parsley
Boiled new potatoes

In large buttered baking dish, arrange fish. Sprinkle with onion, salt and pepper. Combine apple juice, Irish Mist and lemon juice. Pour over fish. Cover. Bake in preheated 350°F oven 15 minutes. Strain liquid. Reserve. Keep fish warm.

In small saucepan, melt butter. Mix in flour. Cook 2 minutes. Stir in fish liquid and cream. Cook until thickened. Pour over fish. Sprinkle with cheese. Place under broiler until browned. Sprinkle with parsley. Serve with potatoes. Serves 4-6.

Reprinted with permission of Heublein.

## Gourmet Peanuts

A 29-page booklet, "It's Easy to be a Gourmet with Peanuts," that lists over 200 recipes for using peanuts and peanut butter in main dishes, soups, salads, breads, sandwiches, sauces, and desserts. Recipes include Pork Chops Caribe, Peanut Rice Casserole and Peanut Butter Cookies.

**Send:** 50ᶜ.
**To:** Oklahoma Peanut Commission #1, P.O. Box D, Madill, OK 73446

## Almonds

Fifty pages of recipes in "The Crazy about Almonds and Chocolate Cookbook" give you dozens of ideas for using these two ingredients in cookies, candies, cakes, breads, soups and main dishes like North African Chicken and Indonesian Barbecued Pork Spareribs.

**Send:** a postcard.
**To:** Almond Board of California, Dept. FS—1, P.O. Box 15920, Sacramento, CA 95813

## Peanut Dishes

A glossy 15-page pamphlet, called "Recipes Using Peanuts: Nutrition in a Nutshell," with dozens of peanut recipes for appetizers like Barbecued Peanuts, main dishes like Indonesian Pork Kabobs, and desserts like Peanut Pralines. Includes nutrition information and storage tips.

**Send:** a 9" self-addressed, stamped envelope.
**To:** Growers Peanut Food Promotions, P.O. Box 1709, Rocky Mount, NC 27801

### North African Chicken

1 chicken (about 3½ lbs.)
Salt and pepper
¾ C slivered almonds
2 T butter
2 t curry powder
1 medium tomato, diced
¾ C cooked rice
½ C dark seedless raisins
2 T minced parsley
½ t cinnamon
½ oz. unsweetened chocolate, shaved or chopped

Sprinkle chicken inside and out with salt and pepper. Saute almonds in butter until golden. Add curry powder; saute 1 minute; remove from heat. Stir in tomato, rice, raisins, parsley, cinnamon, chocolate, ½ teaspoon salt and ½ teaspoon pepper.

Stuff mixture into both chicken cavities. Close with skewers. Tie legs together and wings close to body. Roast at 375° for 1 hour 45 minutes or until tender, basting occasionally with drippings. Makes 4 servings.

Reprinted with permission of the Almond Board of California.

# RECIPES

## Sunflowers

Fifteen pages of information about sunflower oil, which is low in saturated fats, and sunflower seeds, which are high in protein. Includes a handful of recipes for using these products in baked goods like Sunflower Seed Bread and Sunflower Pie. Ask for "Straight from the Sun."

**Send:** 40¢.
**To:** North Dakota Sunflower Council—SFTS, Capitol Bldg., Bismarck, ND 58505

## Bean Dishes

A small foldout, called "Bean Dishes to Brag About," that offers a half dozen special ways to prepare beans, including Barbecue Blackeyes and Mock Enchilada Casserole. You'll also find cooking and soaking tips.

**Send:** a 9″ self-addressed, stamped envelope.
**To:** California Dry Bean Advisory Board, P.O. Box 943, Dinuba, CA 93618

## Dry Beans

A 32-page booklet, "California Ways with California Dry Beans," that lists over 40 different ways to prepare beans. Includes recipes for lima, kidney, garbanzo, blackeye, pink and small white beans. Recipes range from Chili and Baked Beans to Oven Bean Soup with Lamb.

**Send:** $1.00. *7·14·80*
**To:** California Dry Bean Advisory Board, P.O. Box 943, Dinuba, CA 93618

### Old-Fashioned Baked Beans

| | |
|---|---|
| 1 lb. California small white beans | ½ C chopped onion |
| 1 qt. boiling water | ¼ C molasses or honey |
| 1½ t salt | ¼ C brown sugar |
| 1 t dry mustard | ¼ C cider vinegar |
| ½ t fresh ground black pepper | ¼ lb. salt pork, cubed |
| Dash of cayenne or Tabasco | |

Add beans to boiling water; boil 2 minutes, then remove from heat and let soak 1 hour. (Or cold-soak overnight, if you prefer.) Drain beans. Combine dry ingredients and mix with beans. Stir in onion, molasses, brown sugar and vinegar.

Put half of the 6-cup mixture into a 1½-qt. or 2-qt. baking dish or bean pot. Add half the pork, then the rest of beans. Top with remaining pork. Pour in boiling water to top of beans. Cover. Bake at 300° for 6 hours if to be served at once; 5 hours for those to be frozen. Add a little boiling water if needed during baking. Makes 1½ quarts (6 servings).

Reprinted with permission of the California Dry Bean Advisory Board.

18

## Pasta

Recipes for using pasta — spaghetti, macaroni, linguini, rigatoni and many other varieties. The Golden Grain Macaroni Company has a number of pamphlets and foldouts available and will send you some. Ask for "Pasta Recipes."

**Send:** a 9″ self-addressed, stamped envelope.
**To:** Golden Grain Macaroni Co., 1111-139th Ave.—Dept. C, San Leandro, CA 94578

## Pasta Winners

"Twelve Award-Winning Pasta Recipes," a foldout that lists the winners of the third Pasta Recipe Contest. Describes how to make such dishes as Lasagne Mornay, Linguini a La Caruso and Peking Pork Salad.

**Send:** a 9″ self-addressed, stamped envelope.
**To:** The National Macaroni Institute, P.O. Box 336, Palatine, IL 60067

### Linguini a La Caruso

1 lb. chicken livers
6 T butter
1 C sliced mushrooms (fresh or canned)
½ C chopped onion
½ C diced green pepper
2 cloves garlic, minced
1 can (28 oz.) plum tomatoes, cut up
1 can (15 oz.) tomato puree
2 t sweet basil, crushed
2 t oregano, crushed
½ t salt
½ t pepper
12 oz. enriched durum linguini
2 T parsley

Saute the chicken livers in ¼ cup butter until brown; set aside. Saute mushrooms, onion, green pepper and garlic in remaining butter until onions are tender. Add tomatoes and puree; stir in basil, oregano, salt and pepper. Bring to a boil, then lower heat and simmer, uncovered, 30 minutes.

Cook linguini in boiling salted water (2 quarts water plus 1 tablespoon salt) until tender, yet firm, about 10 to 12 minutes; drain. Add sauteed chicken livers to tomato sauce; simmer 5 minutes. Serve sauce over hot linguini. Sprinkle with parsley. Serves 6.

# RECIPES

## Secret Recipes

A 1-page sheet known as "Gloria Pitzer's Secret Recipe Report" with 8 recipes for making all those foods you thought you could only buy from stores, like a certain kind of fried chicken that comes in a bucket and a certain kind of cookie (she calls them Gloreos).

**Send:** a 9″ self-addressed, stamped envelope.
**To:** Gloria Pitzer, P.O. Box 152, St. Clair, MI 48079

## Radio Recipes

A 24-page booklet, called "Aunt Sammy's Radio Recipes" (G215), that reprints some of the recipes first broadcast on a popular radio show of the late 1920's, including Shepherd's Pie and Chicken and Dumplings. This new edition also contains some current favorites. Ask for by name and number.

**Send:** a postcard.
**To:** Publications Division, Office of Governmental and Public Affairs, U.S. Dept. of Agriculture, Washington, DC 20250

## Group Cooking

"Cooking for Small Groups" (AB 370), a 21-page recipe booklet for people who prepare food for small group gatherings. Each recipe, for dishes like Pot Roast, Oven-Fried Chicken, Green Beans with Herbs, or Raisin Bars, yields 25 servings. Ask for by name and number.

**Send:** a postcard.
**To:** Publications Division, Office of Governmental and Public Affairs, U.S. Dept. of Agriculture, Washington, DC 20250

### Wednesday's Chili
(Rich & Meaty)

Brown 1½ lbs. ground beef in 2 T oil till tender. With back of fork, break meat up into tiny rice-like pieces. Put 10-oz. can onion soup through blender on high speed along with half of the browned beef. Blend till it resembles "cement mortar" and return it to the rest of the beef in a 2½-qt. heavy saucepan.

Add 1 t chili powder, 2 t cumin powder, ½ t pepper, 2 T cocoa powder (the secret ingredient . . . ) and 2 cans (15-oz. each) red kidney beans undrained, plus 6-oz. can tomato paste, 15-oz. can tomato sauce. Stir in 2 T packed brown sugar, 1 t vinegar, 6-oz. can V-8 juice. Simmer till all of the ingredients get well acquainted with each other.

Reprinted with permission of Secret Recipes, St. Clair, MI

## Corn Starch

Two colorful 7x10-inch recipe cards from the makers of Argo and Kingsford's corn starch. Each card starts with a basic cooking technique, like making a white sauce or a fruit pie filling, and then shows you how to build on that recipe and prepare more elaborate sauces, gravies, soups and fillings.

**Send:** a postcard.
**To:** Corn Starch Recipes, Dept. CSS—FSC, P.O. Box 307, Coventry, CT 06238

## Soup & Salad

A short recipe foldout from Running Press that reprints 11 recipes from 2 of their cookbooks, the *Big Green Salad Book* and the *Big Blue Soup Book*. Includes recipes for Pear and Leek Soup, Bean Sprout and Mushroom Salad, Dill Sour Cream Dressing, and more.

**Send:** a 9" self-addressed, stamped envelope.
**To:** Running Press—FS, 38 S. 19th St., Philadelphia, PA 19103

## Mustard

A 20-page pamphlet that explains the history of mustard — especially Dijon mustard, which has been produced in France since the 13th century and is now also made in the U.S. by Heublein. The booklet, called "Dijon Mustard, the Third Seasoning," contains dozens of recipes for appetizers, sandwiches, sauces and main dishes.

**Send:** 30ยข.
**To:** The Mustard Information Bureau, Dept. ST, P.O. Box 538, Lenox Hall Station, New York, NY 10021

### Pear and Leek Soup

- 4 T margarine or salad oil
- 2 C chopped leek
- 1 can (1 lb.) pears, packed in juice
- 4 C chicken stock
- ½ t summer savory
- ¼ t salt
- Salt and white pepper to taste
- Croutons

Combine margarine and leek in saucepan. Saute leek for about 3 minutes or until tender. Transfer leek to blender or food processor. Add pears with juice. Blend until smooth. Transfer to saucepan. Add chicken stock, summer savory and salt. Bring to boil. Lower heat. Cover and simmer for about 20 minutes. Add salt and white pepper to taste. Serve soup in warm tureen or warm individual soup bowls. Garnish with croutons. Serves 6.

Reprinted with permission of Running Press.

# RECIPES

## Rice International

A colorful 13-page booklet, called "International Favorites," featuring rice dishes from around the world. Includes recipes for Beef Curry (Pakistan), Chicken and Peas Pilav (Turkey), Chicken Cantonese (China) and 11 more dishes.

**Send:** a postcard.
**To:** Rice Council of America, Dept. FM, P.O. Box 22802, Houston, TX 77027

## Basic Rice

A short foldout, called "Look What's Hiding in Your Cupboard," full of recipes for using rice in a variety of easy side dishes, main dishes and desserts. Recipes include Chili Franks and Rice, Tuna Rice Royale and Rice Au Gratin Supreme.

**Send:** a postcard.
**To:** Rice Council of America, Dept. FM, P.O. Box 22802, Houston, TX 77027

## Rice Salads

A foldout with 8 recipes for using rice instead of potatoes in a variety of salads. Includes recipes like Mandarin Rice Salad and Seafood Rice Salad, plus directions for cooking rice in large or small quantities. Ask for "Rice Salads for any Occasion."

**Send:** a postcard.
**To:** Rice Council of America, Dept. FM, P.O. Box 22802, Houston, TX 77027

### Rice Salads

#### Mandarin Rice Salad

½ C diced green pepper
¾ C sour cream
1 T lemon juice
1 t each seasoned salt and seasoned pepper
3 C cool cooked rice
1 can (16 oz.) Mandarin orange segments, drained
1½ C thinly sliced celery

Blend all ingredients thoroughly. Chill. Serve on salad greens and sprinkle with sliced almonds, if desired. Makes 6 servings.

Reprinted with permission of the Rice Council of America.

#### Seafood Rice Salad

1 pkg. (8 oz.) frozen cooked shrimp
1 can (6½ to 7 oz.) tuna, drained
3 C cool cooked rice
½ C each finely chopped onions and sweet pickles
1½ C thinly sliced celery
¼ C diced pimientos
3 hard-cooked eggs, chopped
1 T lemon juice
1 C mayonnaise

Combine all ingredients and toss lightly. Season to taste. Chill. Serve on salad greens and garnish with tomato wedges. Makes 6 servings.

## Rice Dishes

A recipe foldout, called "Brown Rice," that lists a dozen ways of using brown rice, which takes longer to cook than white rice and has a different flavor and texture. Includes recipes for Vegetarian Rice, Oriental Pancakes with Chinese Sauce, and some nutritional information.

**Send:** a postcard.
**To:** Rice Council of America, Dept. FM, P.O. Box 22802, Houston, TX 77027

## White Rice

Thirteen pages of rice recipes in a booklet called "Success-ful Recipes." Includes over 25 ways to use Success Rice in dishes like Hungarian Beef and Rice, Quick Sweet and Sour Pork, Gourmet Chicken Livers and Rice, and California Pilaf.

**Send:** 25ᶜ.
**To:** Success Recipes, P.O. Box 2636, Dept. FS, Houston, TX 77001

## Brown Rice

A 14-page pamphlet, called "Your Collection of Special Recipes," that describes 12 ways to use brown rice, the unmilled rice that retains a natural brown coating of bran. Recipes range from Stuffed Zucchini and Sherried Mushroom Rice to Old-Fashioned Brown Rice Custard.

**Send:** 25ᶜ.
**To:** Brown Rice Recipes, P.O. Box 2636, Dept. FS, Houston, TX 77001

### Hungarian Beef and Rice

1 bag Success Rice
1½ lbs. round steak
2 T vegetable oil
½ C chopped onion
1 garlic clove, minced
¾ C water
⅓ C catsup

2 T brown sugar
2 T Worcestershire sauce
1 t paprika
½ t dry mustard
1 t salt
1 T cornstarch

Cook bag of rice according to package directions. Drain and keep warm. Cut steak into strips, 2"x½". Brown quickly in hot oil. Add the onion and garlic. Saute another few minutes. Pour off excess fat. Stir in ½ cup water, catsup, brown sugar, Worcestershire sauce, paprika, dry mustard and salt. Cover and simmer 30 minutes.

Combine cornstarch with the remaining water. Stir into the meat mixture. Heat and stir until shiny and thickened. Serve over hot, fluffy rice. Makes 4 servings.

Reprinted with permission of Riviana Foods.

# RECIPES

## Corn Flakes

A 23-page pamphlet with recipes for "Corn Flake Crumbs Cookery." Over 2 dozen ways to use corn flake crumbs in breads, cookies, brownies, pies, cakes, tortes, main dishes and side dishes. Simple, clear instructions and attractive illustrations.

**Send:** a postcard.
**To:** Kellogg Co., Dept. CCS, Battle Creek, MI 49016

## Chex

"The Natural Way to Good Cooking," a 25-page booklet that describes dozens of ways to use Wheat, Rice and Corn Chex in breads, burgers, meat loaf, casseroles, pies and cakes.

**Send:** 3 proofs-of-purchase from any Chex cereal.
**To:** Natural Way to Good Cooking, P.O. PL 14089, Dept. B, Belleville, IL 62222

## Bran Chex

Twenty-five pages of recipes for using Bran Chex, which add fiber to your diet. Try breakfast treats like Sour Cream Coffee Cake, main dishes like Stuffed Cabbage Rolls, and desserts like Southern Pecan Pie. Ask for "The Bran Chex Plan for Good Cooking."

**Send:** 3 proofs-of-purchase from any Chex cereal.
**To:** Bran Chex, P.O. PL 14089, Dept. E, Belleville, IL 62222

### Tangy Meatloaf

½ C catsup
2 T brown sugar
½ t dry mustard
4 t Worcestershire sauce
¼ t garlic powder
1½ t onion powder
2 t seasoned salt
¼ t pepper
1 egg
2 T finely chopped green pepper
1½ C Wheat Chex cereal crushed to ¾ cup
1½ lbs. ground beef

In a large bowl combine catsup, brown sugar and dry mustard. Remove 4 tablespoons of mixture and reserve for topping. To remaining mixture add Worcestershire, garlic and onion powders, salt, pepper and egg. Blend well. Stir in green pepper and Chex. Add ground beef. Mix well.

Shape into loaf in shallow pan. Bake at 350° for 65 minutes. Remove from oven and spread top with reserved catsup mixture. Bake additional 15 minutes. Makes about 6 servings.

Reprinted with permission of Ralston Purina.

# RECIPES

## Cereal Recipes

An assortment of "Cereal Recipes" from the Roman Meal Company. Each foldout shows you how to prepare a variety of breads, desserts and other baked goods with cereal. One foldout describes how to use cereal in meat dishes like Creole Meat Loaf and Beef Mexicana.

**Send:** a postcard.
**To:** Roman Meal Co., Consumer Services, Dept. M, 2101 S. Tacoma Way, Tacoma, WA 98409

## Yeast Recipes

A colorful 23-page booklet, "New and Easy Yeast Recipes," that includes dozens of recipes for breads (like French bread, Garlic bread, and Rye bread), pizza dough, and coffeecakes (like Kolaches and Almond Streusel Coffeecake). Includes tips on baking with yeast.

**Send:** 50¢.
**To:** Cookbooks, Universal Foods Corp., P.O. Box 737, Milwaukee, WI 53201

## Baking Bread

Three bread recipes reprinted from Garden Way Publishing's *Bread Book,* plus information on how to buy the complete book through the mail. Recipes for Sour Cream Banana Bread, Rich White Batter Bread and Mill Hollow Bread.

**Send:** 25¢ plus a 9" self-addressed, stamped envelope.
**To:** Bread Recipes, c/o Garden Way Publishing, Dept. A 268A, Charlotte, VT 05445

### Roman Meal Banana Nut Bread

1⅓ C all-purpose flour
¾ C granulated sugar
2 t baking powder
½ t salt
⅔ C Roman Meal Cereal, instant or regular variety
½ C chopped nuts
1 C mashed bananas (about 2 medium bananas)
½ C milk
⅓ C vegetable oil
2 eggs
1 T lemon juice

In a large bowl mix flour, sugar, baking powder, salt, cereal and nuts. In smaller bowl measure remaining ingredients; beat with fork to mix. Pour into dry ingredients; stir until just blended. Bake in well-greased 9x5x3-inch loaf pan in moderate oven (350°F) about 50 minutes or until pick inserted in center comes out clean. Cool in pan on rack 5 minutes. Remove from pan; cool completely on rack.

© Roman Meal Co.

# RECIPES

## Prizewinners I

Seventeen pages of "Prizewinning Recipes from Red Star's 1st Baking Recipe Exchange," including savory Cheese 'N Rye bread, naturally wholesome Four Grain English Muffins, and sweet Ethiopian Honey Spice Bread. Also contains tips on baking with yeast.

**Send:** 50ᶜ.
**To:** Cookbooks, Universal Foods Corp., P.O. Box 737, Milwaukee, WI 53201

## Prizewinners II

More winners in "The Best of Red Star's 2nd Baking Recipe Exchange" — Norwegian Almond Muffins, Butterscotch Rum Rolls, Onion-Wine Crescents, and 20 more yeast breads, rolls and coffeecakes. Easy-to-follow instructions and tips for baking with yeast.

**Send:** 50ᶜ.
**To:** Cookbooks, Universal Foods Corp., P.O. Box 737, Milwaukee, WI 53201

## Prizewinners III

Still more winners in "The Best of Red Star's 3rd Baking Recipe Exchange" — including recipes for Pita Bread, Easy Croissants, Mexican Pizza, Grated Potato Bread and over 2 dozen more yeast-baked goods.

**Send:** 50ᶜ.
**To:** Cookbooks, Universal Foods Corp., P.O. Box 737, Milwaukee, WI 53201

### Pita Bread

| | |
|---|---|
| 4½ to 4¾ C all-purpose flour | 1½ t sugar |
| 1 pkg. Red Star Instant Blend Dry Yeast | 1½ t salt |
| | 1¾ C water |
| | 2 T oil |

In large mixer bowl, combine 2 cups flour, yeast, sugar and salt; mix well. In saucepan, heat water and oil until warm (120-130°). Add to flour mixture. Blend at low speed until moistened; beat 3 minutes at medium speed. By hand, gradually stir in enough remaining flour to make a firm dough.

Knead on floured surface until smooth and elastic, about 10 minutes. Cover dough with plastic wrap, then a towel. Let rest 20 minutes on board.

Punch down dough. Divide into 12 equal parts. Shape each part into a smooth ball. Place on board, allowing space between each ball. Cover; let rise 30 minutes. Preheat oven to 500°. Roll each ball into a 6-inch circle. Place 3 circles at a time directly onto oven rack. Bake until puffed and top just begins to brown, about 3 minutes. Cool on racks. Yield: 12 Pocket Breads.

Reprinted with permission of Universal Foods.

26

## Using Bread

A large 32-page booklet, "Things to Do with Bread Besides Butter It," that's full of recipes that let you use bread in soups, salads, stuffings, fondues, casseroles and appetizers. Includes a collection of party ideas that kids can help with.

**Send:** a postcard.
**To:** Roman Meal Co., Consumer Services, Dept. M, 2101 S. Tacoma Way, Tacoma, WA 98409

## Quick Baking

An instructive 15-page booklet, called "No-Time-To-Bake Baking Recipes," that tells you how to bake everything from basic breads to elegant desserts in half the usual time. Rolls and sweet goods can be made in an hour, breads in 90 minutes.

**Send:** 50¢.
**To:** Cookbooks, Universal Corp., P.O. Box 737, Milwaukee, WI 53201

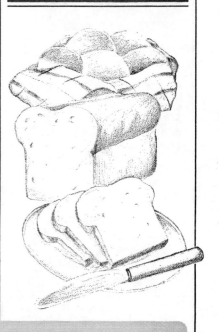

### Swiss Cheese Fondue Casserole

2 T butter or margarine
3 T all-purpose flour
1 t salt
Dash of thyme
1½ C milk
1 C grated process Swiss cheese
2 eggs, separated
1 pint ½-inch soft bread cubes
2 green pepper rings

Melt butter in medium-sized saucepan. Blend in flour, salt and thyme. Add milk; cook until thick. Add cheese; stir until it melts. Gradually blend cheese sauce into beaten egg yolks. Add soft bread cubes; mix well. Beat egg whites until stiff and dry. Fold into cheese mixture. Pour into greased 1-quart casserole. Set casserole in pan of hot water; bake in slow oven (325°F) for 1 hour. Garnish with green pepper rings. Serve immediately. Makes 6 servings.

© Roman Meal Co.

# RECIPES

## Roquefort

A colorful 38-page recipe booklet, called "Roquefort," that tells you how to buy, serve and preserve this unique cheese made of sheep's milk in the south of France. Includes dozens of recipes for dishes like Roquefort Cognac Dip, Potato Salad and Cheese Cake.

**Send:** 25¢.
**To:** Roquefort Assn., Inc., P.O. Box 2908, Grand Central Station, New York, NY 10017

## Danish Cheese

Three short booklets, "Say Danish Cheese Please," "Karoline's Favorite Danish Cheese Recipes," and "Karoline's Danish Blue Cheese Recipes," that tell you how to use Danish cheeses in all sorts of foods — Danablu soup, Danish hamburgers, main dishes, dressings and appetizers.

**Send:** a postcard.
**To:** Royal Danish Consulate General, Danish Information Office, 280 Park Ave., New York, NY 10017

## Roquefort

### Parisien Dip

| | |
|---|---|
| 1 pkg. (8 oz.) cream cheese, softened | 3 T heavy cream |
| 3 oz. Roquefort cheese | 1 t chopped chives |
| | ½ t Worcestershire sauce |

To the softened cheese, add the Roquefort cheese, cream, chopped chives and the Worcestershire sauce. Mix until well blended. Place in a bowl and sprinkle with additional chives. Serve with potato chips. Makes about 1½ cups.

### Basic Dressing

| | |
|---|---|
| 1 C Roquefort | 1 T lemon juice |
| 1 T Worcestershire sauce | ⅔ C salad oil |
| | 2 T vinegar |

Mash cheese with little salad oil. Add Worcestershire sauce, lemon juice, vinegar and balance of oil. Shake well until creamy. Serve on lettuce, cucumbers or endive.

Reprinted with permission of the Roquefort Assn.

## Egg Dishes

A 64-page booklet full of 'Classic Egg Dishes" that lists over 100 recipes. Includes tips on mixing, beating, separating and cooking eggs, plus recipes for appetizers and drinks, salads and dressings, sandwiches, omelets, souffles, and main dishes.

**Send:** $1.00.
**To:** Classic Egg Dishes, Minnesota Egg Council, 2950 Metro Dr., Suite 308, Minneapolis, MN 55420

## Eggs

A whole handful of foldouts, called "Everything You've Always Wanted to Know about Eggs." Includes recipes for omelets, crepes and quiches (try the Sausage Apple Omelet or the Vegetable Quiche), plus various other breakfast or dinner egg dishes.

**Send:** $1.00.
**To:** Missouri Egg Merchandising Council, 319 Eastgate Bldg., Columbia, MO 65201

## Egg Ideas

A collection of "Recipes from the Egg Kitchen," from the Georgia Egg Commission. Includes general cooking instructions, plus tips on making crepes and omelets, pickling eggs, cooking them in the microwave, and so on.

**Send:** 50¢.
**To:** Recipes from the Egg Kitchen, Georgia Egg Commission, Dept. MP, State Farmers' Market, Forest Park, GA 30050

### Scotch Eggs

A coating of sausage and bread crumbs makes a hearty snack of hard-cooked eggs. After cooking to a golden turn, they can be eaten hot or cold. Scotch eggs are a traditional companion to a mug of ale or beer.

¾ lb. bulk pork sausage
12 hard-cooked eggs
1 egg, beaten
⅓ C fine dry bread crumbs
Fat for deep frying

Divide sausage into 12 equal portions (1 oz. each). Shape each portion into patty and wrap completely around 1 hard-cooked egg, pressing edges together to seal. Dip sausage-wrapped eggs in beaten egg, then roll in bread crumbs until completely coated. Cook eggs in preheated 375°F deep fat until golden brown and heated through, 7 to 9 minutes. Drain on absorbent paper. Serve hot or cold. Makes 6 servings.

Reprinted with permission of the Minnesota Egg Council.

# RECIPES

## Chocolate Ideas

Recipes for using Ghirardelli chocolate products — powder, chips and bars — in a variety of cookies, cakes, brownies, sauces and other desserts. Ask for "Chocolate Recipes" and you'll receive any one of a number of pamphlets or foldouts available.

**Send:** a 9″ self-addressed, stamped envelope.
**To:** Golden Grain Macaroni Co.—1111-139th Ave.—Dept. C, San Leandro, CA 94578

## Chocolate Favorites

A 32-page booklet, called "Hershey's Favorite Recipes," that describes how to use cocoa, baking chocolate, chocolate chips and syrup in dozens of ways. Includes recipes for cakes, frostings, pies, muffins, waffles, pancakes and beverages.

**Send:** a postcard.
**To:** Hershey Foods Corp., Educational Materials Dept., Hershey, PA 17033

## Microwave

Two dozen recipes in a small booklet called "Microwave Recipes from Hershey's Chocolate Company." Describes how to make hot cocoa, fudge, brownies, pound cake, pudding and other chocolate desserts in the microwave.

**Send:** a postcard.
**To:** Hershey Foods Corp., Educational Materials Dept., Hershey, PA 17033

### Butter-Almond Crunch

1½ C butter or margarine
1¾ C sugar
3 T light corn syrup
3 T water
1½ C Hershey's Mini Chips
1¾ C chopped almonds

Lightly butter a 13x9x2-inch pan. Spread 1 cup Mini Chips evenly over bottom; set aside. Spread almonds in shallow pan or on baking sheets; toast at 350°, stirring occasionally, for 7 to 8 minutes or until golden brown. Set aside.
Melt butter or margarine in a 2½-qt. saucepan; blend in sugar, corn syrup and water. Cook over medium heat, stirring constantly, to hard-crack stage (300°F). Remove from heat; stir in 1½ cups of the toasted almonds. Immediately spread mixture evenly over Mini Chips in pan, being careful not to disturb chips. Quickly sprinkle remaining ¼ cup almonds and ½ cup Mini Chips; score into 1½-inch squares, if desired. Cool; cover pan and store overnight. Remove from pan; break into pieces. Store in tightly covered container. About 2¼ pounds candy.

Reprinted with permission of Hershey.

## Rice Desserts

A small foldout, called "Rice Desserts," with about a dozen recipes for using rice in a variety of desserts. Includes basic advice on cooking rice, plus recipes for puddings, custards, cheesecake and special desserts like Raspberry Rice A L'Amande.

**Send:** a postcard.
**To:** Rice Council of America, Dept. FM P.O. Box 22802, Houston, TX 77027

## Frozen Desserts

A 19-page booklet full of the "Secrets of Making Frozen Desserts." Includes instructions for making basic vanilla ice cream (you need a hand-cranked or an electric machine), plus recipes for preparing fancier ice creams, mousses and sherbets.

**Send:** 50ᶜ.
**To:** White Mountain Freezer Inc., Lincoln Ave. Extension, Winchendon, MA 01475

## Cookies

A set of recipe sheets, called "Christmas Cookies," that tell you how to make the 3 kinds of cookies that are traditional in all Danish homes at Christmastime — Brown Cookies, Peppernuts, and Smalls, which are a kind of deep-fried cookie.

**Send:** a postcard.
**To:** Royal Danish Consulate General, Danish Information Office, 280 Park Ave., New York, NY 10017

### Raspberry Rice a L'Amande

1 C uncooked rice
2 C water
1 t salt
¼ C sugar
1 t vanilla extract
½ pint heavy cream, whipped

2 pkgs. (10 oz. each) frozen raspberries, thawed
1 T cornstarch
3-4 drops red food coloring

Combine rice, water, salt and sugar. Bring to a boil, stir once, cover, reduce the heat, and simmer 15 minutes, or until rice is tender and liquid is absorbed. Remove from heat; stir in vanilla. Cool. Fold whipped cream into cooled rice. Drain liquid from raspberries into a small saucepan. Blend in cornstarch; cook over low heat until thick.

Add raspberries and food coloring. Stir gently to prevent breaking up berries. Chill. Alternate layers of rice mixture and raspberries in serving bowl or parfait glasses. Makes 8 to 10 servings.

Reprinted with permission of the Rice Council of America.

# RECIPES

## Peach Ice Cream

A short foldout full of recipes for "Peach Ice Creams." If you like to make your own ice cream, you'll want to learn how to make almond-flavored Southern Peach Ice Cream, Fat-Free Fresh Peach Ice Cream, Peach Sherbet and a half dozen other varieties.

**Send:** a 9″ self-addressed, stamped envelope.
**To:** L. A. Barbour, National Peach Council, P.O. Box 1085, Martinsburg, WV 25401

## Peach Pies

"Fresh Peach Pies," a short recipe foldout that tells you how to make a basic pie with fresh peaches, and then goes to describe half a dozen variations, including French Crumb Fresh Peach Pie and Deep Dish Fresh Peach Pie.

**Send:** a 9″ self-addressed, stamped envelope.
**To:** L. A. Barbour, National Peach Council, P.O. Box 1085, Martinsburg, WV 25401

## Peach Preserves

A short foldout, called "Peachy Preserves," full of recipes for making jams, preserves and butters using fresh peaches. Recipes include Peach Rum Jam and Cantaloupe-Peach Marmalade.

**Send:** a 9″ self-addressed, stamped envelope.
**To:** L. A. Barbour, National Peach Council, P.O. Box 1085, Martinsburg, WV 25401

### Deep Dish Fresh Peach Pie

5 C sliced fresh peaches (about 8 medium-size)
2 T flour
¾ C sugar
½ t cinnamon
1 t butter
1 pkg. ready-to-bake refrigerated cookie dough

Mix peaches, flour, sugar, cinnamon. Put into 8-inch square baking pan. Cut butter into small pieces over top of peaches. Arrange ¼-inch slices of cookie dough in rows over top of peaches. Bake at 350° for 1 hour. Cool about 2 hours before serving. Top with whipped cream, ice cream or pass a pitcher of cream. Makes 6 to 8 servings.

Reprinted with permission of the National Peach Council.

## Glazes & Butters

Two recipe foldouts from Globe Products give you some ideas for using Continental Strawberry Glaze, Lekvar Prune Butter and Golden Apricot Butter in sauces, cakes, pies, tortes and other desserts and dishes.

**Send:** a postcard.
**To:** Globe Products Co., Inc., Consumer Division, P.O. Box 1927, Clifton, NJ 07015

## Fruit Sauces

An 18-page booklet, called "Vintage Fruit Sauces," that tells you how to make lightly fermented fruit sauces using yeast. It also includes dozens of recipes for using this topping to prepare meat dishes like Vintage Sauced Ribs, vegetables like Vintage Stuffed Squash, plus various salads and breads.

**Send:** 50ᶜ.
**To:** Cookbooks, Universal Foods Corp., P.O. Box 737, Milwaukee, WI 53201

## Rice Syrup

A 19-page recipe booklet, "The Yinnies Brand Rice Syrup Cookbook," that shows you how to make a variety of desserts and sweet treats using Yinnies Rice Syrup. This thick syrup is made from rice and a tiny bit of malted barley — no sugars or chemicals are added.

**Send:** a postcard.
**To:** Free Yinnies Cookbook, Chico-San, Dept. FSC, P.O. Box 1004, Chico, CA 95927

### Barbecued Chicken —Apricot Sauce

2 lbs. chicken
½ C Apricot Butter
¼ C light molasses
½ C catsup
1 medium onion, chopped
4 whole cloves
Dash garlic salt
1 T lemon juice
1 T salad oil

1 T vinegar
½ t prepared mustard
¼ t salt
¼ t pepper
½ t Worcestershire sauce
1 T butter
¼ t Tabasco

Combine ingredients and boil for 5 minutes; heat oven to 325°; cover chicken with aluminum foil in shallow pan and roast 1 hour, pouring off excess grease occasionally; remove foil; pour off excess fat and pour sauce over chicken. Roast chicken at 400°, uncovered, until glazed and tender.

Reprinted with permission of Globe Products Co.

# RECIPES

## Popcorn

A short foldout, "Recipes for Pop Corn Lovers," with over a dozen different ideas for preparing popcorn. Includes basic tips on preparing a batch of popcorn, plus recipes for popcorn balls, popcorn bars, peanut butter popcorn, blue cheese popcorn and much more.

**Send:** a postcard.
**To:** Jolly Time Pop Corn, American Pop Corn Co., P.O. Box 178, Dept. M, Sioux City, IA 51102

## Fresh Garlic

A small foldout from the Fresh Garlic Association, called "Garlic and Vegetables Go Together." Includes buying and storing tips, plus recipes for about 10 garlic and vegetable dishes, like Stir Fried Vegetables and Cauliflower with Garlic Oil.

**Send:** a 9″ self-addressed, stamped envelope.
**To:** Fresh Garlic Assn., c/o Caryl Saunders Associates, P.O. Box 9106, San Rafael, CA 94902

## Vegetables

A short recipe foldout from the canners of Veg-All Mixed Vegetables. Ask for a "Veg-All Recipe Book," and you will receive their current selection of ideas for using vegetables in salads, soups, casseroles, quiches, or meat and vegetable pies.

**Send:** a postcard.
**To:** The Larsen Co.—VRB, P.O. Box 1563, Green Bay, WI 54305

### Snow Peas Canton

1 T peanut oil
4-5 cloves fresh California garlic, minced
½ lb. Chinese pea pods, ends trimmed, strings removed
1 can (5 oz.) sliced bamboo shoots, drained

1 can (8 oz.) water chestnuts, drained and sliced
¼ C canned or fresh chicken broth
2 t soy sauce
1 t cornstarch
2 t water

Heat oil in a large skillet or wok. Saute garlic until light brown. Add peas, bamboo shoots and water chestnuts. Stir-fry 1 minute. Add chicken broth and soy sauce. Cover and cook another minute. Combine cornstarch and water. Stir into skillet. Cook over high heat until sauce thickens and appears glossy, about 1 minute. Yield: 4 servings.

Reprinted with permission of the Fresh Garlic Assn.

## Yam Dishes

A small foldout with over a dozen recipes for various "Yam Dishes," including Sweet Potato Biscuits and Sweet Potato Custard Pie, where yams are the main ingredient, and various ham dishes and casseroles, where yams are an important addition.

**Send:** a postcard.
**To:** North Carolina Yam Commission, Inc., P.O. Box 12005, Raleigh, NC 27605

## Yams

Four foldouts about sweet potatoes, each with recipes for dishes like Bayou Bread, Peach Glazed Ham, Louisiana Yams and Acadian Candied Yams. Ask for one or more of the following: "The Versatile Ones," "Louisiana Yam-mates," "Louisi-Yam-a Recipe Roundup" or "A Southern Yam-o-Rama."

**Send:** a postcard.
**To:** Louisiana Sweet Potato Commission, P.O. Box 113, Opelousas, LA 70570

## Sweet Potatoes

A short booklet, called "Cooking with Sweet Potatoes," that describes 36 ways of doing just what its title says. Includes recipes for Sweet Potatoes with Pork Roast, Sweet Potato Stuffing and Yam Tarts. Plus other tips on using sweet potatoes.

**Send:** 30¢ plus a 9" self-addressed, stamped envelope.
**To:** Harold H. Hoecker, Sweet Potato Council of the U.S., Inc. 5023 Iroquois St., College Park, MD 20740

### Sweet Potato Biscuits

1 C all-purpose flour
3 t baking powder
½ t salt
3 T fat

1 C cooked, mashed sweet potatoes
About ¼ C milk

Sift together the dry ingredients. Chop in the fat. Add the mashed sweet potatoes and mix well. Add gradually only enough milk to make a soft dough. Knead a few strokes. Roll dough ⅓ inch thick. Cut in rounds and place on a baking sheet. Bake in a hot 450°F. oven 12 to 15 minutes. Serve hot.

Reprinted with permission of the North Carolina Yam Commission.

# RECIPES

## Apricots

A glossy booklet, the "California Apricot Growers' Favorite Recipes," that lists over 50 ways to use apricots in main dishes, soups, salads, breads and desserts. Also a "Nutrition Calculator" that lets you compare the nutritional value of various fruits.

**Send:** a postcard.
**To:** California Apricot Advisory Board, 1295 Boulevard Way, Walnut Creek, CA 94595

## Pineapples

A short foldout that shows you how to use "Everything But the Can" when you're cooking with canned pineapple. Contains recipes that have you use both the pineapple and the syrup (but no more sugar) in dishes like Mandarin Muffins, Pineapple Spinach Salad and Red Hot Stir Fry.

**Send:** a postcard.
**To:** Castle & Cooke Foods, Free Stuff: Everything But the Can, P.O. Box 7758, San Francisco, CA 94119

## Coconut

A short foldout, "Coconut Creations," that tells you how to buy coconuts, crack their shells, and use their meat in a variety of ways. Recipes range from Decadent Coconut Cream Chicken to Frozen Yogurt and Frosty Pina Coladas.

**Send:** a postcard.
**To:** Castle & Cooke Foods, Free Stuff: Coconut Creations, P.O. Box 7758, San Francisco, CA 94119

### Cantonese/ Apricot Rice

3 T butter or margarine
1 C uncooked rice
½ C chopped onion
¼ t ground ginger
2 C chicken broth or bouillon

1 C diced dried California apricots
⅓ C dark seedless raisins
½ C chopped celery
½ C salted peanuts
Salt

Melt butter in large skillet; add rice and onion and saute until golden brown. Add ginger, chicken broth, apricots, raisins and celery. Simmer, covered, about 10 minutes or until rice is almost tender. Mix peanuts into rice mixture and season to taste with salt. Serve as accompaniment to roast pork or poultry. Makes 6 servings.

Reprinted with permission of the California Apricot Advisory Board.

## Applesauce

Two 8½x11-inch sheets that provide about a dozen recipes for using applesauce in dishes like Apple Spoon Bread, Breakfast Apple Crisp and Savory Beans and Franks. Ask for "Winning Ways" and "Creative Meals."

**Send:** a 9″ self-addressed, stamped envelope.
**To:** Virginia State Apple Commission, P.O. Box 718, Dept. FS, Staunton, VA 24401

## Apples

Two recipe leaflets from the Washington Apple Commission. Each leaflet includes at least a half dozen tips on using Golden Delicious apples in salads, fritters, cakes, pies, cookies and casseroles.

**Send:** a 9″ self-addressed, stamped envelope.
**To:** Apple Recipes, P.O. Box 550, Wenatchee, WA 98801

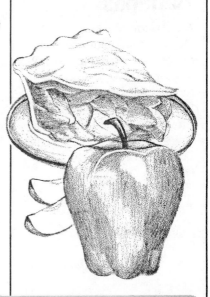

### Golden Delicious Apple Crisp

| Golden Delicious Apple Crisp | | Topping | |
|---|---|---|---|
| 5 Golden Delicious, medium size | ¼ t salt | ½ C granulated sugar | ½ C butter |
| 1 t lemon juice | 1 t cinnamon | ½ C sifted flour | ½ C chopped nuts |
| 1 t grated lemon rind | ½ C sugar | | |

Wash, pare, core and slice apples into a bowl. Add lemon juice, rind, cinnamon, sugar. Blend until apples are well coated; put into 6-cup shallow baking dish, buttered. Cover with crumb topping.

Crumble together, pack over apples. Bake in 350° oven for 45 minutes. Serve with cream, whipped cream or ice cream. Serves 8.

Reprinted with permission of the Washington Apple Commission.

# RECIPES

## Bananas

A 30-page booklet, "The Dole Banana Bonanza," full of recipes for using bananas in every meal. Includes recipes for Greek Pita Sandwiches, Caribbean Beef Stew, Whole Grain Banana Cake, Daiquiris and at least 30 more dishes. Also contains storing tips.

**Send:** a postcard.
**To:** Castle & Cooke Foods, Dept. Q: Free Stuff for Cooks, P.O. Box 7758, San Francisco, CA 94119

## Raisins

"Raisins — Everything Under the Sun," a 36-page booklet that collects over 80 raisin recipes for quick and yeast breads, cakes, cookies, salads, sauces, souffles and puddings. Recipes include Dutch Apple Raisin Pie and Irish Soda Bread.

**Send:** 25¢.
**To:** Raisins — Everything Under the Sun, California Raisin Advisory Board, P.O. Box 5172, Dept. FS, Fresno, CA 93755

## Raisin Desserts

Two short foldouts on raisins, "Hearty and Healthy Raisin Recipes" and the "Cookie Bookie of Rare Raisin Recipes." Each includes a half dozen recipes for baked goods like Raisin Carrot Cake, Speckled Brown Bread and Hannah Kent's Raisin Cookies.

**Send:** a postcard.
**To:** California Raisin Advisory Board, P.O. Box 5335, Dept. FS, Fresno, CA 93755

### Irish Soda Bread

2 C flour
1 T sugar
1½ t baking powder
1 t soda
¼ t salt
¼ C butter or
    margarine,
    softened

¾ C raisins
1½ t caraway seeds
    (optional)
1 C buttermilk
1 egg slightly beaten
    with 1 T water

Sift flour, sugar, baking powder, soda and salt into a large mixing bowl. Cut in butter with a pastry blender until mixture resembles coarse meal. Stir in raisins and caraway seeds. Add buttermilk; blend to moisten the dry ingredients.

Turn dough onto floured board; knead for several minutes until smooth. Form dough into a round ball and place on greased baking sheet. Flatten ball until dough is about 1½" high; brush top and sides with egg/water mixture. Cut a ½" deep cross in top of bread with sharp knife.

Bake at 375° for 30 to 40 minutes or until toothpick inserted in center comes out clean. Transfer to wire rack to cool; brush top with butter or margarine and cover with cloth. Makes 1 round soda bread.

Reprinted with permission of the California Raisin Advisory Board.

# Dates

A 14-page booklet, called "A Modern Almanac of Date Recipes," that contains over a dozen new and different ways to use dates in everyday cooking. Includes recipes for Holiday Meatballs, Chicken Curry, Banana Date Muffins and more.

**Send:** a 9″ self-addressed, stamped envelope.
**To:** Bordo Products Co., 2825 N. Sheffield Ave., Chicago, IL 60657

# Blueberries

A short foldout full of "Blueberry Classics." Includes buying, storing and using tips, plus about 20 recipes gathered from all over the world, ranging from Georgia Blueberry Pancakes to Blueberry Liqueur.

**Send:** 15¢.
**To:** North American Blueberry Council, P.O. Box 38, Tuckahoe, NJ 08250

# Soy Pancakes

A short foldout of "Pancake and Crepe Recipes" that call for Fearn Soya's SOY/O Pancake Mixes, soybean and flour products made without sugar. Also includes recipes for Cheese Blintzes, Ginger Waffles, and Biscuits.

**Send:** a 9″ self-addressed, stamped envelope.
**To:** Fearn Soya Foods, Dept. MP—PC, 4520 James Pl., Melrose Park, IL 60160

## Holiday Meatballs

### Meatballs

2 lbs. lean ground beef
1 T seasoned salt
1 T brown sugar
¾ C water
2 t lemon peel
1 8-oz. package Bordo imported diced dates

### Sauce

3 10¾ oz. cans condensed tomato soup
1½ soup cans of water
¾ C brown sugar
3 T lemon juice
1 8-oz. package Bordo imported diced dates

Mix ground beef and remaining meatball ingredients until well blended and dates are dispersed through mixture. Set aside. Place tomato soup in a large (5-6 quart), heavy saucepan. Add water, brown sugar and lemon juice. Mix well. Bring to a slow boil, uncovered, over medium heat. Then simmer. Stir occasionally.

Using about 1 teaspoon of meat mixture, shape with hands into balls and drop into simmering liquid. Repeat until meat mixture is used. Simmer meatballs in sauce, uncovered, 15 minutes. Add dates. Mix carefully. Simmer an additional 15 minutes, stirring every 5 minutes, until sauce thickens. Serves 8-10 as a hearty appetizer.

Reprinted with the permission of Bordo.

# RECIPES

## Natural Foods

A copy of the "Chico-San Products and Recipe Booklet," which contains descriptions of Chico-San's natural food products (whole grains, cereals, seeds, beans, seasonings, etc.). Includes recipes for tempura, curried vegetables, and whole wheat spaghetti.

**Send:** a postcard.
**To:** Free Catalog and Recipes, Chico-San, Dept. FSC, P.O. Box 1004, Chico, CA 95927

## Health Recipes

A sample copy of "Gayelord Hauser Gourmet Health Recipes and Beauty Secrets," a booklet full of dozens of recipes for breakfasts, soups, sauces, dressings and main dishes. Includes information about a potato diet, with sample menus and recipes.

**Send:** a 9″ self-addressed, stamped envelope.
**To:** Gayelord Hauser Recommended Products, P.O. Box 09398, Dept. FS, Milwaukee, WI 53209

## Bulgur

A colorful booklet, "Enjoy Bulgur," that shows you how to use bulgur, a crushed wheat food, in a variety of ways. Bulgur can be eaten alone or mixed with fruit, vegetables, salads, meat or fish. Includes cooking tips and some nutritional information.

**Send:** a 9″ self-addressed, stamped envelope.
**To:** Nutrition Education Program, Nebraska Wheat Committee, Dept. FSFC, P.O. Box 94912, Lincoln, NE 68509

### Tabooli

**Salad**

1½ C bulgur (dry)
1 bunch green onions
1 green pepper
1 cucumber
3 tomatoes, peeled and seeded
1 bunch parsley

**Dressing**

½ C vegetable (or olive) oil
½ C lemon juice
1 t salt

Cover bulgur with hot water. Soak at least 2 hours. This can be done in the refrigerator. Drain excess water and squeeze reconstituted bulgur. Chop all vegetables very fine. Mix with bulgur. Add dressing and mix well. Let stand for 2 hours before serving. Keeps well in refrigerator.

Reprinted with permission of the Nebraska Wheat Committee.

## Wheat & Corn

"Wheat Germ and Corn Germ Recipes" — foldouts full of ideas for using 2 of Fearn Soya's products, both of which are made without preservatives or artificial ingredients. Can be used to prepare casseroles, loaves, souffles and sauces.

**Send:** a 9″ self-addressed, stamped envelope.
**To:** Fearn Soya Foods, Dept. MP—WC, 4520 James Pl., Melrose Park, IL 60160

## Wheat Germ

A little foldout, "Ways with Wheat Germ," that describes the nutritional value of Kretschmer Wheat Germ, and tells how to store it and use it. Includes 8 recipes.

**Send:** a 9″ self-addressed, stamped envelope.
**To:** Wheat Germ Recipes, Consumer Communications —FS, International Multifoods, 1200 Multifoods Bldg., Minneapolis, MN 55402

## Vegetarian Meals

A set of foldouts full of "Vegetarian Recipes" that describe how to make various meatless meat dishes using Fearn Soya's sunflower, sesame and Brazil nut mixes. Includes recipes for Sesame Shepherd's Pie and Zucchini-Burger Bake.

**Send:** a 9″ self-addressed, stamped envelope.
**To:** Fearn Soya Foods, Dept. MP—VB, 4520 James Pl., Melrose Park, IL 60160

### Spicy Apple Wheat Germ Muffins

1½ C unsifted all-purpose flour
½ C Kretschmer Regular or Sugar & Honey Wheat Germ
3 t baking powder
½ t salt
¾ t cinnamon
¼ t nutmeg
½ C sugar
¼ C softened butter or margarine
2 eggs
½ C milk
1 C peeled, finely chopped apple
½ C currants or raisins

Combine flour, wheat germ, baking powder, salt and spices on wax paper. Stir well to blend. Cream sugar, butter and eggs thoroughly. Add blended dry ingredients to creamed mixture alternately with milk. Blend well. Stir in apples and currants. Fill paper-lined or greased muffin-pan cups about ⅔ full. Bake at 400° for 20-25 minutes. Serve warm with butter. Yield: 1 dozen muffins.

Reprinted with permission of International Multifoods.

# RECIPES

## Vegetarian Dishes

A 28-page booklet, called "A Taste of Nature Cookbook," with 59 simple vegetarian recipes. The booklet answers questions about natural foods and shows you how to make main dishes, soups, salads and sandwiches without meat or with meat substitutes.

**Send:** $1.00.
**To:** Professional Health Media Services, Inc., P.O. Box 922 MP—011, Loma Linda, CA 92354

## Grains & Legumes

A 4-page excerpt from *The Oats, Peas, Beans, & Barley Cookbook,* a comprehensive vegetarian cookbook. Reprints 6 recipes (including Lentil Roast and Hurry-Up Hearty Hash), and explains how to get the whole book by mail.

**Send:** a postcard.
**To:** Woodbridge Press Publishing Co., P.O. Box 6189, Santa Barbara, CA 93111

## Soybeans

Foldouts full of "Soya Food Recipes" — ideas for using Fearn Soya's soybean powder and granules in a variety of soups, stews, casseroles, cereals, baked goods and beverages. The granules are also an excellent meat extender.

**Send:** a 9" self-addressed, stamped envelope.
**To:** Fearn Soya Foods, Dept. MP—SF, 4520 James Pl., Melrose Park, IL 60160

### Hurry-up Hearty Hash

2 C cooked brown rice
½ C sauteed onions
½ C chopped celery
½ C chopped Brazil nuts
¼ C brewers flake yeast (with B-12)

2 T oil
½ t salt
1/8 t garlic powder
2 T soy sauce
2 C shredded raw potatoes

Measure and combine all ingredients except potatoes. Wash potatoes, scrubbing off only part of the skin with plastic or steel scouring pad. Cut out spots. Shred potatoes and add. Mix.

Spoon in thin layers into unoiled skillet or baking dish. Medium-hot, 350°F. Cover. Let cook 10 minutes. Turn. Stir. Cover. Cook 10 or 15 minutes longer. Yield: 6 servings.

Reprinted with permission of the Woodbridge Press Publishing Co.

# KITCHEN GUIDES

# KITCHEN GUIDES

## Cutting Beef

A short foldout, called "Cut a Little — Save a Lot," that describes how to save up to 30% on beef prices by being your own butcher. Includes instructions on selecting and cutting various cuts of beef to make the most efficient use of them.

**Send:** a 9″ self-addressed, stamped envelope.
**To:** Cut a Little, Oregon Beef Council, 400 S.W. Broadway, Portland, OR 97205

### CUTTING A PORTERHOUSE
Cut along both sides of T-bone and separate into two steaks, the top loin (larger of the two) and the tenderloin. These are both very tender cuts of beef and can be broiled or barbecued just the way you like them!

## Roasts

A 16-page pamphlet, "How to Buy Beef Roasts" (G146), that's a consumer guide to roasts. Tells how beef is graded, describes various cuts, and suggests how much to allow per serving. Ask for by name and number.

**Send:** a postcard.
**To:** Publications Division, Office of Governmental and Public Affairs, U.S. Dept. of Agriculture, Washington, DC 20250

### RUMP ROAST
This is a very flavorful cut, but it is less tender than the rib and it also contains a considerable amount of bone. In Prime, Choice, and Good grades, it can be oven-roasted; pot roast the lower grades. Allow at least a half-pound of bone-in rump per person and about a third of a pound per person for boneless rump.

## Beef & Veal

A complete 38-page guide to using "Beef and Veal in Family Meals" (G118), full of information about buying, storing and cooking beef and veal. Includes temperature and time tables, charts of cuts, and dozens of recipes, each of which yields 6 servings. Ask for by name and number.

**Send:** a postcard.
**To:** Publications Division, Office of Governmental and Public Affairs, U.S. Dept. of Agriculture, Washington, DC 20250

### BROILING TIPS
- Put aluminum foil in bottom of broiler pan to simplify cleaning.
- Grease broiler grid to help prevent meat from sticking.
- Turn meat by sticking fork into the fat, not the lean, or use tongs.
- Broil frozen meat at a low temperature to prevent surface from charring before interior thaws. Increase cooking time.

# KITCHEN GUIDES

## Steaks

A 16-page pamphlet, "How to Buy Beef Steaks" (G145), that's a consumer guide to steak, from tenderloin to bottom round. Explains the various USDA grades and provides a chart of the various cuts. Ask for by name and number.

**Send:** a postcard.
**To:** Publications Division, Office of Governmental and Public Affairs, U.S. Dept. of Agriculture, Washington, DC 20250

### SIRLOIN STEAK
The sirloin is a large steak, which makes it suitable for family or party fare. It contains several different muscles and varies in size, shape and bone size. To get the most for your money, look for one with a small amount of bone (wedge or round bone); but for maximum tenderness, pick out a sirloin with a long, flat bone.

## Buying Lamb

A 16-page pamphlet, "How to Buy Lamb" (G195), that's a consumer guide to lamb, from loin chops to leg of lamb. Includes an explanation of USDA grades, a chart of cuts, and some cooking tips. Ask for by name and number.

**Send:** a postcard.
**To:** Publications Division, Office of Governmental and Public Affairs, U.S. Dept. of Agriculture, Washington, DC 20250

### LAMB RIB CHOPS
Cut from the rib (rack), these tender chops are delicious broiled, pan-broiled or panfried. For best results, have rib chops cut at least 1 inch in thickness. Approximate cooking time for 1 inch — 12 minutes; 1½ inches — 18 minutes; and 2 inches — 22 minutes.

## Lamb

A complete 21-page guide to using "Lamb in Family Meals" (G124) that offers a wealth of information about buying, storing and cooking lamb. Includes temperature and time tables, a chart of lamb cuts, and about a dozen recipes, each of which yields 6 servings. Ask for by name and number.

**Send:** a postcard.
**To:** Publications Division, Office of Governmental and Public Affairs, U.S. Dept. of Agriculture, Washington, DC 20250

### SUGGESTED STORAGE PERIODS

| Fresh Lamb: | Refrig. Days | Freezer Months |
|---|---|---|
| Chops and Steaks | 3 to 5 | 6 to 9 |
| Ground Lamb | 1 to 2 | 3 to 4 |
| Roasts | 3 to 5 | 6 to 9 |
| Stew Lamb | 1 to 2 | 3 to 4 |
| Variety Meats | 1 to 2 | 3 to 4 |

# Lamb Cookery

"Lamb Cookery Basics" and "Lamb Cuts," a foldout and a chart that offer a number of tips about buying, storing, roasting, broiling, frying and braising lamb. Includes a time and temperature table and a lamb cuts chart.

**Send:** 25ᶜ.
**To:** Lamb Education Center, Dept. MP A—127 B—172, 200 Clayton St., Denver, CO 80206

# Buying Pork

A 9x4-inch cardboard sliding scale, "The Pork Buyer's Guide," that shows the various cuts of pork, the servings per pound for each cut, and cooking procedures, times and temperatures.

**Send:** a 9″ self-addressed, stamped envelope.
**To:** Recipes, Missouri Pork Producers Assn., 922 Fourth St., #10E, Boonville, MO 65233

# Pork

A complete 33-page guide to using "Pork in Family Meals" (G160), full of buying, storing and cooking tips. Includes time and temperature tables, charts of cuts, and dozens of recipes, each of which yields 6 servings. Ask for by name and number.

**Send:** a postcard.
**To:** Publications Division, Office of Governmental and Public Affairs, U.S. Dept. of Agriculture, Washington, DC 20250

### COOKING TIMES FOR ROASTS

Lamb roasts are palatable cooked anywhere from 140°F internal temperature to well done at 170°F. It is desirable to allow a roast to stand in a warm place for 15 or 20 minutes after removal from the oven to make slicing easier. During this period, the roast will continue to cook inside and the internal temperature will rise from 5° to 10°.

### COOKING METHODS

Most pork cuts can be cooked by dry heat methods (roasting, broiling, panfrying and panbroiling), but some cuts do require braising or cooking in liquid. To insure maximum flavor and juiciness and minimum cooking loss, roast fresh pork to an internal temperature of 170°F.

### BRAISING TIPS

- Floured meat browns better than unfloured meat.
- Chops and steaks can be breaded with fine, dry bread or cracker crumbs.
- Meats that have considerable fat and that are not breaded or floured can be browned without added fat.

# KITCHEN GUIDES

## Poultry

A short foldout, "How to Buy Poultry" (G157), that's a consumer guide to chicken, turkey, duck, goose and game hen. Explains USDA grades and offers use and storage tips. Ask for by name and number.

**Send:** a postcard.
**To:** Publications Division, Office of Governmental and Public Affairs, U.S. Dept. of Agriculture, Washington, DC 20250

### POULTRY TIPS
Young tender-meated classes are most suitable for barbecuing, frying, broiling or roasting. Young chickens may be labeled — young chicken, Rock Cornish game hen, broiler, fryer, roaster or capon. Mature, less-tender-meated classes may be preferred for stewing, baking, soups or salads. Mature chickens may be labeled — mature chicken, old chicken, hen, stewing chicken or fowl.

## Tuna

Four pages of "Facts on Tuna" full of all sorts of information. Discusses the 4 main tuna species, how tuna is caught and packed, and what its nutritional content is. Includes a few serving tips.

**Send:** a postcard.
**To:** Castle & Cooke Foods, Facts on Tuna, P.O. Box 7758, San Francisco, CA 94119

### TUNA PACKING
**Solid White** — When the label says "solid white" it means the can contains large pieces of albacore tuna. Solid white albacore has an excellent mild flavor and creamy white color.
**Chunk Light** — Small, bite-size pieces of fish go into cans labeled "chunk light." Chunk light tuna is made from skipjack, yellowfin or bluefin. It has a darker color and fuller flavor than albacore.

## Fresh Foods

A short, general guide, called "The Joy of Fresh," that presents a number of facts and tips about the nutrition, economy, convenience, storage, and preparation of fresh fruits and vegetables.

**Send:** a 9" self-addressed, stamped envelope.
**To:** United Fresh Fruit and Vegetable Assn., N. Washington at Madison, Alexandria, VA 22314, Attn: Information Dept.

### COOKING TIPS
Remember the 3 R's of nutrient conservation when cooking fresh fruits and vegetables to obtain all the delicious wholesomeness: 1) reduce the amount of water used, 2) reduce the cooking time, and 3) reduce the amount of exposed surfaces by limiting the amount of cutting, paring and shredding.

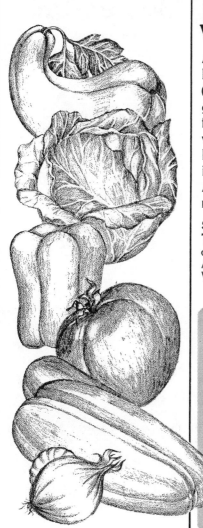

## Fresh Vegetables

A short pamphlet, "How to Buy Fresh Vegetables" (G143), that's a consumer guide to fresh vegetables, from asparagus to watercress. Tells what to look for and what to avoid, in simple, clear language. Ask for by name and number.

**Send:** a postcard.
**To:** Publications Division, Office of Governmental and Public Affairs, U.S. Dept. of Agriculture, Washington, DC 20250

### CUCUMBERS
**Look for:** cucumbers with good green color which are firm over their entire length. They should be well-shaped and well-developed, but should not be too large in diameter. Good cucumbers typically have many small lumps on their surfaces. They may also have some white or greenish-white color and still be top quality.

## Vegetable Care

A short guide, called "Fresh Vegetable Selection and Care," to over 30 kinds of vegetables — from artichokes to turnips. Tells you what to look for when buying and how to store to keep fresh. Also includes 2 general vegetable recipes.

**Send:** a 9″ self-addressed, stamped envelope.
**To:** United Fresh Fruit and Vegetable Assn., N. Washington at Madison, Alexandria, VA 22314, Attn: Information Dept.

### ONIONS
Choose onions that are clean and firm. The skins should be dry, smooth and crackly. Avoid onions with wet, soggy necks, soft or spongy bulbs, which indicate decay. Keep at room temperature, cool, in a well-ventilated area. May be refrigerated; above all, keep dry. They can be stored 3 to 4 weeks.

# KITCHEN GUIDES

## Canned Vegetables

A 24-page booklet, "How to Buy Canned and Frozen Vegetables" (G167), that's a consumer guide to processed vegetables, from artichokes to tomatoes. Explains USDA grades, labeling regulations and styles. Ask for by name and number.

**Send:** a postcard.
**To:** Publications Division, Office of Governmental and Public Affairs, U.S. Dept. of Agriculture, Washington, DC 20250

### TIPS ON CONTAINERS
When you buy canned vegetables, be sure the cans are not leaking or swelled or bulged at either end. Bulging or swelling indicates spoilage. It may be dangerous even to taste the contents. Small dents in cans do not harm the contents. Badly dented cans, however, should be avoided.

## Mushrooms

Four pages of "Facts on Mushrooms" full of all sorts of information. Discusses where and how mushrooms grow; how to buy, clean and store them properly; and what their nutritional content is.

**Send:** a postcard.
**To:** Castle & Cooke Foods, Facts on Mushrooms, P.O. Box 7758, San Francisco, CA 94119

### CLEANING MUSHROOMS
When you prepare fresh mushrooms just brush away clinging soil with a damp cloth or soft brush. Since mushrooms grow in pasteurized soil there's no need to peel, soak, scrub or wash them. If desired, rinse them quickly and gently *just* before using. Rough handling can reduce their delicate flavor and texture.

## Iceberg Lettuce

A colorful foldout, called "The Main Attraction," for lettuce-lovers. Includes tips on buying, cleaning and storing Iceberg lettuce, plus ideas for using it in salads, main dishes and snacks. Also contains recipes for homemade mayonnaise and various dressings, including French and Hot Bacon.

**Send:** a 9" self-addressed, stamped envelope.
**To:** California Iceberg Lettuce Commission, P.O. Box 3354, Monterey, CA 93940

### LETTUCE TIPS
- Use the outer leaves from the head of western Iceberg lettuce as a lid to keep that leftover casserole moist when reheating in the oven.
- Cover vegetables with a leaf or two while cooking. You'll need very little water and preserve valuable vitamins.

# KITCHEN GUIDES

## Buying Fruit

A short guide, called "Fresh Fruit Selection," full of tips for buying and storing over 2 dozen kinds of fresh fruit, from apples to watermelons. Also describes peak buying periods for each kind, and provides a few general recipes.

**Send:** a 9″ self-addressed, stamped envelope.
**To:** United Fresh Fruit and Vegetable Assn., N. Washington at Madison, Alexandria, VA 22314, Attn: Information Dept.

## Fresh Fruit

A 24-page pamphlet, "How to Buy Fresh Fruits" (G141), that's a consumer guide to fruit, from apples to tangerines. Tells what to look for and what to avoid, in simple, clear language. Ask for by name and number.

**Send:** a postcard.
**To:** Publications Division, Office of Governmental and Public Affairs, U.S. Dept. of Agriculture, Washington, DC 20250

## Processed Fruit

A 24-page pamphlet, "How to Buy Canned and Frozen Fruits" (G191), that's a consumer guide to processed fruit, from apples to strawberries. Explains USDA grades, and offers storing and using advice. Ask for by name and number.

**Send:** a postcard.
**To:** Publications Division, Office of Governmental and Public Affairs, U.S. Dept. of Agriculture, Washington, DC 20250

### PEARS
Color varies according to variety. Cinnamon russeting on surface won't affect quality. Pears generally require additional ripening at home. Hold at room temperature until stem end yields to gentle pressure, then refrigerate. Year-round availability due to different varieties.

### WATERMELONS
If you want to buy an uncut watermelon, here are a few appearance factors which may be helpful in guiding you to a satisfactory selection. The watermelon surface should be relatively smooth; the rind should have a slight dullness (neither shiny nor dull); the ends of the melon should be filled out and rounded; and the underside, or "belly," of the melon should have a creamy color.

### CANNED PEACHES
Two types of canned peaches are available: clingstone and freestone. Clingstone peaches have a firm and smooth texture and clean-cut edges. Freestone peaches have a softer texture and raggedy edges. Both kinds are yellow to yellow-orange, except for the seldom-seen white freestone.

# KITCHEN GUIDES

## Pineapple

Four pages of "Facts on Pineapple" full of all sorts of information. Discusses how and where pineapple is grown, how it's graded by the USDA, how it's processed and canned, and what its nutritional content is.

**Send:** a postcard.
**To:** Castle & Cooke Foods, Facts on Pineapple, P.O. Box 7758, San Francisco, CA 94119

### HARVEST
The pineapple plant bears its first fruit 18 to 22 months after planting. By this time, the plant has grown to approximately 3 feet in height and 4 feet in width. Each plant produces a single 4-to-5-pound pineapple. The peak season for processing pineapple is between May and August.

## Pineapple Primer

A short 10-page booklet, called "Patricia Collier's Pineapple Primer," with tips on storing, cutting and growing fresh pineapple. Also includes tips on using pineapple with other foods, plus 5 recipes to get you started.

**Send:** a postcard.
**To:** Castle and Cooke Foods, Dept. PP/Free Stuff for Cooks, P.O Box 7758, San Francisco, CA 94119

### STORING FRESH PINEAPPLE
Pineapple develops dark spots from changes in temperature. So if it was chilled when you got it at the grocery store, keep it chilled at home. And if it wasn't chilled at the grocery store, keep it at room temperature. But either way, slice it and enjoy it as soon as possible.

## Bananas

Six pages of "Facts on Bananas" full of all sorts of information. Discusses how and where bananas grow, how to buy and store them properly, and what their nutritional content is.

**Send:** a postcard.
**To:** Castle & Cooke Foods, Facts on Bananas, P.O. Box 7758, San Francisco, CA 94119

### STORING BANANAS
1) Take them out of the plastic produce bag and keep them at room temperature. This way bananas will continue to ripen. 2) To store bananas for a longer time keep them in your refrigerator. Their peel will darken, but the fruit inside will be ripe and fresh. 3) Bananas will keep for the longest possible time in the freezer. Just mash the fruit with a little lemon juice and freeze it in an air-tight container.

## California Strawberries

A short foldout, called "California Strawberries," with information on how to buy and store strawberries, plus tips on how to use them to prepare glazes, jams, dips, pies, cakes and favorites like milkshakes and sodas.

**Send:** a postcard.
**To:** California Strawberry Advisory Board, P.O. Box 269, Watsonville, CA 95076.

### CLEANING STRAWBERRIES
Never wash strawberries or remove caps until just before using. Washing removes the natural protective outer layer. The caps protect the strawberries and help preserve flavor, texture and nutrients.

## Grapes

A 4-page foldout, called "Grapes: The Natural Snack," with tips on using grapes as snacks and in meals, a brief history of grapes and a list of the 14 varieties available in California. Also includes a few recipes for dishes like Grape Harvest Streusel and Marinated Chicken Veronique.

**Send:** a 9″ self-addressed, stamped envelope.
**To:** California Table Grape Commission, The Natural Snack, P.O. Box 5498, Fresno, CA 93755

### GRAPE TIPS
- For a summer breakfast, fill cantaloupe halves with fresh California grapes and top with a dollop of fruit-flavored yogurt, a sprinkling of wheat germ or crunchy cereal.
- Leftover chicken? Prepare your favorite chicken salad mixture. Add a handful of seedless or halved and seeded grapes and chopped nuts to see how far your leftovers can go.

## Raisins

A small foldout, called "Questions You've Been Raisin . . . and Our Answers," full of information about the history of raisins and the various types available; also includes tips for storing, handling and using raisins and a chart describing their nutritional content.

**Send:** a postcard.
**To:** California Raisin Advisory Board, P.O. Box 5335, Dept. FS, Fresno, CA 93755

### STORING RAISINS
Heat and air can cause raisins to dry out, and humid conditions will cause the sugar in the fruit to crystallize. Therefore, after the package has been opened, raisins should be put in a sealed container or a plastic bag and refrigerated. Raisins will retain their flavor, color and nutritive value up to 2 years if stored in the refrigerator.

# KITCHEN GUIDES

## Egg Buying

A short foldout, "How to Buy Eggs" (G144), that's a consumer guide to egg grades and sizes. Provides nutrition, storing and using information. Ask for the publication by name and number.

**Send:** a postcard.
**To:** Publications Division, Office of Governmental and Public Affairs, U.S. Dept. of Agriculture, Washington, DC 20250

### EGG FACTS
- To insure best eating quality, eggs should be cooked with low to moderate heat. High temperatures and overcooking toughen eggs.
- For hardcooked eggs, use your oldest eggs. Very fresh eggs when hardcooked may be harder to peel.

## Dairy Products

A 16-page pamphlet, "How to Buy Dairy Products" (G201), that's a consumer guide to milk, cream, butter, cheese, yogurt and ice cream. Explains USDA grades and provides storage tips. Ask for by name and number.

**Send:** a postcard.
**To:** Publications Division, Office of Governmental and Public Affairs, U.S. Dept. of Agriculture, Washington, DC 20250

### DAIRY TIPS
- For maximum shelf life, do not return unused cream from a pitcher to its original container. Store it separately in the refrigerator.
- Unopened fruit-flavored yogurt may be frozen up to 6 weeks. To defrost, let the yogurt stand at room temperature about 3 hours.

## Eggs

A complete 29-page guide to using "Eggs in Family Meals" (G103), full of information about buying, storing and preparing eggs in a variety of ways. Includes dozens of recipes for egg salads, sandwiches, main dishes and desserts, each of which yields 6 servings. Ask for by name and number.

**Send:** a postcard.
**To:** Publications Division, Office of Governmental and Public Affairs, U.S. Dept. of Agriculture, Washington, DC 20250

### POACHING EGGS
Break eggs into a saucer or custard cup, one at a time, then slip them into gently boiling, salted water — enough water to cover the eggs in a shallow pan. Reheat water to simmering, take pan from heat, cover. Let stand 5 minutes, or until eggs are of desired firmness. Remove eggs from water and sprinkle with salt and pepper.

# Yogurt

The story of yogurt in a 15-page booklet called "Yogurt and You." Discusses how it's made, what its nutritional value is, and how you can make use of it in sauces, dressings, marinades, desserts and main dishes.

**Send:** a 9" self-addressed, stamped envelope.
**To:** Dorothy R. Young, Dannon Milk Products, Dept. FSC, 22-11 38th Ave., Long Island City, NY 11101

---

### YOGURT TIPS
Summertime Soup — a great cold soup idea for hot summer days. Simply mix 2 cups of Dannon Plain Yogurt with 1 can of chilled condensed tomato soup. If that's too heavy, thin with milk. Season this lightly with celery salt and onion salt, sprinkle with freshly chopped olives and parsley.

# Beer

"The Home Brewing Handbook" — a complete guide to making your own beer. Includes a short history of brewing, a discussion of the kinds of ingredients and equipment you'll need, and step-by-step instructions for making lager, dark beer and stout.

**Send:** a postcard.
**To:** Duane Imports Ltd., 508 Canal St., Dept. FSC, New York, NY 10013

---

### BEER
Traditional beer making depends on three simple natural processes: 1) the malting of barley to convert the grain into a liquid malt, 2) the natural action of yeast on the malt sugar to make alcohol, and 3) the preserving essence of the hops that are added to the barley malt extracts.

# Nuts

A complete 14-page guide to using "Nuts in Family Meals" (G176), full of information about all kinds of nuts from almonds to walnuts. Includes buying and storing tips plus recipes for using nuts in main dishes, salads, soups and desserts. Ask for by name and number.

**Send:** a postcard.
**To:** Publications Division, Office of Governmental and Public Affairs, U.S. Dept. of Agriculture, Washington, DC 20250

---

### COOKING TIP
Mix $2/3$ C sour cream, $1/4$ t grated onion, $1/2$ t salt and 1/8 t white pepper. If desired, add 1 t horseradish and 1/8 t ground dill seed. Chill. Stir in $1/3$ C chopped, toasted almonds or pecans. Serve over hot baked potatoes, asparagus spears, sliced cucumbers or beet salad.

# KITCHEN GUIDES

## Almonds

A short foldout, called "Almonds for Goodness Sake," that describes the varieties of almonds and their nutritional content. Includes tips on roasting, toasting, blanching, chopping and storing almonds, and suggests a number of uses.

**Send:** a postcard.
**To:** Almond Board of California, Dept. FS—2, P.O. Box 15920, Sacramento, CA 95813

### BLANCHING ALMONDS
Place shelled, whole natural almonds in a saucepan. Cover with water and bring to a boil over high heat. Remove from heat immediately and drain. When cool enough to handle, press each almond between your thumb and finger; the skin will slip off easily.

## Cooking Peanuts

A short foldout, "All About Cooking Peanuts," that provides simple directions for storing peanuts, removing their skins, and roasting or french frying them. Includes recipes for Southern Peanut Pie, Peanut Brittle and Parmesan Peanuts.

**Send:** a 9" self-addressed, stamped envelope.
**To:** Growers' Peanut Food Promotions, P.O. Box 1709, Rocky Mount, NC 27801

### PEANUT TIPS
- Chili Peanuts: to 1 C roasted peanuts add ¼ t chili powder and 1/8 t paprika. Stir over very low heat until peanuts are hot.
- Garlic Peanuts: to 1 C roasted peanuts add ¼ t garlic powder. Stir well to blend.
- Nature's Munch: combine 1 C roasted peanuts, 1 C sunflower seeds, 1 C raisins. Enjoy.

## Peanuts

Two recipe pamphlets, "How to Cook a Peanut" and "Recipes from Your Oklahoma Peanut Commission," that show you dozens of ways to cook and use peanuts. Includes information on blanching, french frying, oil roasting, dry roasting, sugar coating and storing peanuts, plus all sorts of recipes.

**Send:** a 9" self-addressed, stamped envelope.
**To:** Oklahoma Peanut Commission #2, P.O. Box D, Madill, OK 73446

### STORING PEANUTS
To maintain best eating quality, store peanuts in a cool, dry place. Vacuum packs keep indefinitely unopened. In the shell, peanuts keep approximately 9 months in the refrigerator and indefinitely if frozen in a tightly closed container at 0°F or lower. Shelled peanuts keep approximately 3 months in the refrigerator and indefinitely if frozen in a tightly closed container at 0°F or lower.

## Using Rice

A large-size 4-page foldout about rice that emphasizes its nutritional content and discusses how to cook and use it in a variety of dishes. Includes recipes for breakfast, lunch and dinner. Ask for "American Rice . . . in the Diet."

**Send:** a postcard.
**To:** Rice Council of America, Dept. FM, P.O. Box 22802, Houston, TX 77027

### COOKING YIELDS OF RICE
- 1 C uncooked regular milled rice yields 3 or more cups.
- 1 C uncooked parboiled rice yields 3 to 4 cups.
- 1 C uncooked brown rice yields 3 to 4 cups.
- 1 C pre-cooked rice yields 1 to 2 cups.

## Pasta Primer

A short foldout, called the "Pasta Primer," full of information about spaghetti, macaroni and noodles. Explains how pasta is made, what its nutritional content is, and how to buy, store and cook it. Includes a few recipes for simple pasta dishes.

**Send:** a 9″ self-addressed, stamped envelope.
**To:** The National Macaroni Institute, P.O. Box 336, Palatine, IL 60067

### COOKING PASTA
Gradually add 8 ounces of the pasta product along with 1 T of salt to 3 quarts of rapidly boiling water so that water continues to boil. Cook uncovered, stirring occasionally, until tender. Drain in colander. Caution: Don't overcook! Cook only "al dente" (tender to the tooth). Rinse pasta after draining **only** when making salads.

## Soybean Meals

A complete 26-page guide to using "Soybeans in Family Meals" (G208), full of information about various soybean products, their nutritive value, and their many uses. Includes recipes for main dishes, soups, salads, breads and sandwiches. Ask for by name and number.

**Send:** a postcard.
**To:** Publications Division, Office of Governmental and Public Affairs, U.S. Dept. of Agriculture, Washington, DC 20250

### SOYBEAN OIL
Soybeans are rich in polyunsaturated oil, which is extracted for commercial use. Many commercial vegetable oils contain soybean oil. Processed soybean oil is light in color, has a mild flavor and can be used as oil in any recipe. Soybean oil keeps best at refrigerator temperature after opening.

# KITCHEN GUIDES

## Bean Primer

A large colorful foldout packed with information about dry beans — descriptions of the 12 varieties of Western-grown beans; shopping, storing and cooking tips; plus a handful of recipes for using them (including recipes for chili, baked beans, and vegetarian chowder). Ask for "A Primer on Bean Cookery."

**Send:** a 9″ self-addressed, stamped envelope.
**To:** California Dry Bean Advisory Board, P.O. Box 943, Dinuba, CA 93618

### COOKING TIPS
- Simmer beans slowly. Cooking too fast can break skins.
- A tablespoon of oil prevents foaming.
- Acid slows down cooking. Add tomatoes, vinegar, etc., last.
- Add 1/8 to 1/4 teaspoon baking soda (no more) per pound of beans when cooking in hard water to shorten cooking time.

## Blackeye Beans

A 15-page booklet, called "Blackeyed Beauty," that tells the story of blackeye beans in an imaginative way. Includes a selection of 6 recipes for dishes like Blackeye Beans Creole and Blackeye Appetizer Salad, plus tips for storing, soaking and using the economical blackeye bean.

**Send:** a 9″ self-addressed, stamped envelope.
**To:** California Dry Bean Advisory Board, P.O. Box 943, Dinuba, CA 93618

### BLACKEYE TIPS
- As every good Deep South cook knows, blackeyes are great (fresh or dried) as a vegetable side dish when cooked with a little cured pork to add flavor.
- Blackeyes make a hearty and zesty bean salad or appetizer when marinated in your favorite salad dressing.

## Garnishes

An 8-page booklet, called "All About Garnishes," that shows you how to turn inexpensive foods into attractive garnishes for appetizers, main dishes, desserts, soups, sandwiches and salads. Includes descriptions of some of the Ekco kitchen tools that could help you prepare these garnishes.

**Send:** a 9″ self-addressed, stamped envelope.
**To:** Ekco Housewares Co., Eductional Services Dept., 9234 W. Belmont Ave., Franklin Park, IL 60131

### MEAT ROLL-UPS
To make lunch meat roll-ups, the meat slices are spread with softened cream cheese, rolled and held together with a small skewer or toothpick. After chilling, they are cut into bite-size portions. Roll-ups may be made also with bread or lettuce or cabbage leaves replacing the meat.

## Cutlery

A long illustrated foldout that discusses "How to Choose and Care for Household Cutlery." Includes a description of different styles of knives, blade shapes and cutting edges; also shows you how to use, sharpen and care for knives.

**Send:** 25¢.
**To:** W. R. Case & Sons Cutlery Co., 20 Russell Blvd., Bradford, PA 16701

### CLEANING KNIVES

After use, all knives should be washed off and hand dried thoroughly, particularly if they have been used on fruit or salty foods, which can affect stainless as well as non-stainless blades and may ruin finish if allowed to dry on the blade. They can be washed in a dishwasher, but the high pressure of the water will dull the blade of all knives by knocking them against other items or rack while washing them.

## Buying Cookware

"The Buyer Be-Aware Guide," an informative 26-page booklet that explains how to buy and take care of dinnerware, glassware, flatware and cookware. Two glossaries define basic cookware and glassware terms.

**Send:** $1.00.
**To:** The China Closet, 6807 Wisconsin Ave., Dept. FSC, Chevy Chase, MD 20015

### CARE OF GLASSWARE

Ideally, stemware should be hand washed. The recommended procedure is soaking stemware in hot soapy water in a sink lined with a terry towel, rinsing carefully and standing to dry upside down on a cloth towel. However, if you do insist on the dishwasher, glasses should be placed so that they do not touch each other and cannot fall over.

# KITCHEN GUIDES

## Cookware

A small foldout, called "Get a Handle on Cookware and Small Appliances," that discusses the pros and cons of different cooking materials, and provides tips for using your cookware safely and efficiently. Also includes some product information from Farberware.

**Send:** a 9" self-addressed, stamped envelope.
**To:** Get a Handle on Cookware and Small Appliances, Dept. PIC, Farberware, 1500 Bassett Ave., Bronx, NY 10461

### STAINLESS STEEL
**Pros:** Very durable, attractive, easy to clean. Doesn't react with food to affect nutrients or flavor. Non-porous, smooth surface resists stains, acids, alkalies.
**Cons:** Poor heat conductor; may develop hot spots which cause food to stick or burn.

## Metal Cookware

A large 26-page booklet, called "Consumer Guide to Metal Cookware and Bakeware," full of all sorts of tips about buying cooking utensils, a discussion of various cookware materials and a list of questions and answers often asked about metal cookware.

**Send:** 50ᶜ.
**To:** Metal Cookware Manufacturers Assn., P.O. Box J, Dept. MP, Walworth, WI 53184

### ALUMINUM
One of the primary reasons aluminum cookware has become so popular is that it is an excellent conductor of heat. Because of this quality, heat spreads quickly and evenly across the bottom, up the sides and across the cover to completely surround the food being cooked.

## Thermometers

A 20-page booklet, called "Cooking with Taylor Thermometers," that describes the uses of a variety of microwave, oven, and freezer thermometers. Also includes handy charts of recommended cooking, baking, deep frying and freezing temperatures.

**Send:** a postcard.
**To:** Taylor Instrument—CIP, Sybron Corp., Advertising—Dept. FSC, Arden, NC 28704

### TEMPERATURE
The National Livestock and Meat Board, representing all large meat packers, has proven through extensive research that meat cooked slowly at low temperature is more tender, juicier, more flavorful, more uniformly cooked and more nutritious. Their research has also proven cooking time is only an approximation, whereas a meat thermometer is an accurate guide to the degree of doneness.

## Microwave Cookery

A 16-page introduction to microwave cookery, called "Richard Deacon Gets You Started." Full of tips for using a microwave to warm milk, melt cheese, toast almonds, etc., plus recipes and menus for 3 days full of meals.

**Send:** a 9" self-addressed, stamped envelope (use 28¢ worth of stamps).
**To:** Thermador/Waste King, 5119 District Blvd., Los Angeles, CA 90040, Attn: Advertising Dept. No. FS

### MICROWAVE TIPS
- Soften cold bacon slices 15-20 seconds on High in the package; let stand 3-5 minutes. Slices will separate easily for cooking.
- To liquify honey turned to sugar, heat 30-45 seconds on High.
- Soften 1 cup of hard brown sugar by adding a slice of white bread or an apple wedge and heating, covered, 30-45 seconds on High.

## Microwave Radiation

A 6-page pamphlet from the FDA about "Microwave Oven Radiation." Discusses how microwave ovens work and what the Federal safety standards are. Offers tips to consumers on the proper and safe use of microwaves.

**Send:** a postcard.
**To:** Consumer Information Center, Dept. 553 H, Pueblo, CO 81009

### SAFE MICROWAVE OPERATION
- Examine a new oven for evidence of shipping damage.
- Never operate an oven if the door does not close firmly or is bent, warped or otherwise damaged.
- Never insert objects through the door grill or around the door seal.
- Never turn the oven on when empty.

## Convection Cooking

A short foldout, "Your Guide to Baking, Broiling, Roasting," that introduces convection ovens. They use a fan to force hot air around food, so that foods can be cooked faster and at lower temperatures. Includes cooking tips and recipes.

**Send:** a 9" self-addressed, stamped envelope.
**To:** Rival Manufacturing Co., P.O. Box 8028—CO, Kansas City, MO 64129

### COOKING TIME COMPARISON

Beef Sirloin Tip Roast (4 lbs.)

| | |
|---|---|
| **Conventional Oven** | 2 to 2½ hours at 325° |
| **Rival Convection Oven** | 1½ to 1¾ hours at 300° |

# KITCHEN GUIDES

## Clay Cookery

A long foldout, called "Cook in Clay — the Romertopf Way," that describes the complete process of cooking with Romertopf clay pots. Includes cooking, serving and cleaning tips, plus over a dozen recipes, like Fish Fillets Romertopf and Country Chicken.

**Send:** a 9″ self-addressed, stamped envelope.
**To:** Margaret Meyer, Reco International Corp.—MP, P.O. Box 951, Port Washington, NY 11050

### COOKING PROCESS
The Romertopf Clay Pot is made of a special porous material and is unglazed so that it can "breathe" during the entire cooking process. By soaking the casserole in water before cooking, the pores are filled with water forming a slight moist haze inside the pot. When baked at 450° temperatures, the steam mingles with the natural juices of the pot's contents to penetrate all the inner fibres of meats, fish or vegetables.

## Food Guide

A large 92-page booklet called "Family Fare: A Guide to Good Nutrition" (G1), that offers all sorts of information about food. Includes a daily food guide, tips on meal planning, buying and storing advice, a list of cooking terms and dozens of recipes. Ask for by name and number.

**Send:** a postcard.
**To:** Publications Division, Office of Governmental and Public Affairs, U.S. Dept. of Agriculture, Washington, DC 20250

### VEGETABLE BUYING
**Asparagus** — Stalks should be tender and firm; tips should be close and compact. Choose the stalks with little white — they are more tender. Use asparagus promptly — it toughens rapidly.
**Broccoli** — Look for small flower buds on compactly arranged heads with good green color. Avoid yellowing, soft or spreading heads.

## Food Safety

A short 10-page introduction to "Keeping Food Safe to Eat" (G162) that supplies information about storing, handling, cooking, freezing and canning food properly. Includes a table that outlines the causes, symptoms and ways of preventing bacterial illnesses. Ask for by name and number.

**Send:** a postcard.
**To:** Publications Division, Office of Governmental and Public Affairs, U.S. Dept. of Agriculture, Washington, DC 20250

### COOKING FROZEN FOOD
You can cook frozen meat, poultry or fish without thawing, but you must allow more cooking time to be sure the center of the meat is properly cooked. Allow at least one and a half times as long to cook as required for unfrozen or thawed products of the same weight and shape. Undercooked foods may not be safe to eat.

# KITCHEN GUIDES

## Storage

A 12-page guide to "Storing Perishable Foods in the Home" (G78) that discusses in clear and simple language the storage needs of various foods, from bread to vegetables. Tells where to put food, what temperature to store it at, and how long you can store it safely. Ask for by name and number.

**Send:** a postcard.
**To:** Publications Division, Office of Governmental and Public Affairs, U.S. Dept. of Agriculture, Washington, DC 20250

### STORING CHEESES

**Hard cheeses** such as Cheddar, Parmesan and Swiss. Keep in the refrigerator. Wrap tightly to keep out air. Stored this way, hard cheeses will keep for several months. Cut off mold if it develops on the surface of the cheese.

**Soft cheeses** such as cottage, cream and Camembert. Store tightly covered. Use cottage cheese within 5 to 7 days, others within 2 weeks.

## Jams and Jellies

A 34-page booklet full of information on "How to Make Jellies, Jams and Preserves at Home" (G56). Includes a discussion of the ingredients and equipment necessary, general tips on making and storing jellied products, and dozens of recipes. Ask for by name and number.

**Send:** a postcard.
**To:** Publications Division, Office of Governmental and Public Affairs, U.S. Dept. of Agriculture, Washington, DC 20250

### DEFINITIONS

**Jelly** is made from fruit juice; the product is clear and firm enough to hold its shape when turned out of the container. **Jam,** made from crushed or ground fruit, tends to hold its shape but generally is less firm than jelly. **Preserves** are whole fruits or large pieces of fruit in a thick syrup, often slightly jellied.

# KITCHEN GUIDES

## Canning Basics

"Home Canning Basics," an 8-page booklet that's a condensation of the 30th edition of the Ball Blue Book. It covers the basics of home canning; contains recipes for sauces, juices, jellies, pickles and relishes; and includes tips that will help you avoid common problems.

**Send:** a 9" self-addressed, stamped envelope.
**To:** Ball Corporation, Consumer Affairs Dept. FS, 345 High St., Muncie, IN 47302

### CANNING TIP
Some fruits like apples, apricots, pears and peaches tend to darken while being canned. This can be counteracted by soaking the fruit in commercial ascorbic acid mixture or in a mixture of 2 T each vinegar and salt to 1 gallon water.

## Canned Meat

Twenty-four pages of advice about the "Home Canning of Meat and Poultry" (G106). Instructions on how to prepare meat and poultry, process it in a pressure cooker, pack it in cans or jars, seal the containers, and store it safely. Ask for by name and number.

**Send:** a postcard.
**To:** Publications Division, Office of Governmental and Public Affairs, U.S. Dept. of Agriculture, Washington, DC 20250

### SPOILAGE
- Immediately destroy any canned meat that has spoiled. Burn it or dispose of it where it cannot be eaten by humans or animals.
- Check the contents as you open the container. Spurting liquid, off-color, and color changes in meats are danger signals.

## Canned Produce

A 32-page booklet about the "Home Canning of Fruits and Vegetables" (G8). Includes a discussion of general canning procedures, plus specific advice for canning fruits, tomatoes and pickled vegetables, from asparagus to sweet potatoes. Ask for by name and number.

**Send:** a postcard.
**To:** Publications Division, Office of Governmental and Public Affairs, U.S. Dept. of Agriculture, Washington, DC 20250

### STORING CANNED FOOD
Properly canned food stored in a cool, dry place will retain optimum eating quality for at least a year. Canned food stored in a warm place near hot pipes, a range, or a furnace, or in direct sunlight may lose some of its eating quality in a few weeks or months, depending on the temperature.

## Freezing Poultry

A 29-page guide to the "Home Freezing of Poultry and Poultry Main Dishes" (AB 371). Detailed discussions of how to package and freeze uncooked and cooked poultry, plus recipes for main dishes that can be frozen. Each recipe yields 24 servings. Ask for by name and number.

**Send:** a postcard.
**To:** Publications Division, Office of Governmental and Public Affairs, U.S. Dept. of Agriculture, Washington, DC 20250

### FREEZING TIP
It is convenient to freeze combination foods containing poultry in 8- or 9-inch-square metal pans or other ovenproof dishes. If you line the pan with freezer wrap you can freeze the food right in the pan, and put it back in the freezer for storage.

## Frozen Food

A short 6-page guide to the "Home Care of Purchased Frozen Foods" (G69) that outlines how to buy and store frozen foods, and discusses refreezing and defrosting. Includes a table that lists maximum home-storage periods for various foods. Ask for by name and number.

**Send:** a postcard.
**To:** Publications Division, Office of Governmental and Public Affairs, U.S. Dept. of Agriculture, Washington, DC 20250

### STORAGE PERIODS — FROZEN FOODS (at 0°)

| Food | Months |
|---|---|
| Orange Juice | 12 |
| Beans | 8 |
| Corn | 8 |
| Peas | 8 |
| Apple Pie (unbaked) | 8 |
| Pork Chops | 4 |
| Cut-up Chicken | 9 |
| Ice Cream | 1 |

## Freezing Meals

A 22-page booklet full of information about "Freezing Combination Main Dishes" (G40). Contains recipes for main dishes like baked beans and lasagne that are suitable for freezing, plus tips for preparing your oven recipes for freezing. Ask for by name and number.

**Send:** a postcard.
**To:** Publications Division, Office of Governmental and Public Affairs, U.S. Dept. of Agriculture, Washington, DC 20250

### FREEZING TEMPERATURES
The freezer temperature should be 0°F or below. Unfavorable changes in eating quality take place in foods stored at temperatures above 0°F. Slow growth of microorganisms may occur at temperatures above 10°F, causing food to lose color, flavor, characteristic texture and nutritive value.

# KITCHEN GUIDES

## Freezing Meat & Fish

A complete 23-page guide to "Freezing Meat and Fish in the Home" (G93), full of information about cutting and boning meat, cleaning and dressing fish, and wrapping, freezing, storing and thawing both. Ask for by name and number.

**Send:** a postcard.
**To:** Publications Division, Office of Governmental and Public Affairs, U.S. Dept. of Agriculture, Washington, DC 20250

### WRAPPING MEAT AND FISH
Wrap meat and fish to be frozen in moisture-vapor-resistant coverings to make the package airtight and prevent drying. Place 2 layers of waxed paper between individual chops, steaks and fillets so that individual frozen pieces can be separated easily, then wrap in freezer paper.

## Freezing Produce

A 46-page guide to the "Home Freezing of Fruits and Vegetables" (G10) that discusses what kinds of foods can be frozen, how to prepare and pack them, what kinds of containers to use, and what else you need to know to freeze fruits and vegetables. Ask for by name and number.

**Send:** a postcard.
**To:** Publications Division, Office of Governmental and Public Affairs, U.S. Dept. of Agriculture, Washington, DC 20250

### FREEZER LOADING
Put no more unfrozen food into a home freezer than will freeze within 24 hours. Usually this will be about 2 or 3 pounds of food to each cubic foot of its capacity. Overloading slows down the rate of freezing, and foods that freeze too slowly may lose quality or spoil. For quickest freezing, place packages against freezing plates or coils and leave a little space between packages so air can circulate freely.

## Freezing Beef

A handy foldout, called "Getting the Most from Freezer Beef Buys," that tells you how to buy beef in quantity to store in your freezer. Discusses how much beef to buy, how to determine its quality, how to have it cut, how to wrap it, and how much it's going to cost.

**Send:** a 9″ self-addressed, stamped envelope.
**To:** Minnesota Beef Council, 2950 Metro Dr., Suite 111, Minneapolis, MN 55420

### STORAGE PERIODS — FROZEN BEEF (at 0°)

| Classification | Time |
| --- | --- |
| Beef (fresh) | 6 to 12 months |
| Veal (fresh) | 6 to 9 months |
| Ground Beef | 3 to 4 months |
| Beef for Stew | 3 to 4 months |
| Cooked Beef | 2 to 3 months |
| Processed or Cured Beef Products | 2 weeks |

# NUTRITION INFORMATION

# NUTRITION INFORMATION

# NUTRITION INFORMATION

## Nutrition Needs

A bright colorful introduction to food and nutrition called "Food is More Than Just Something to Eat" (G216). Includes a basic discussion of the major nutrients, plus information about the nutritional needs of people of all ages. Ask for by name and number.

**Send:** a postcard.
**To:** Publications Division, Office of Governmental and Public Affairs, U.S. Dept. of Agriculture, Washington, DC 20250

## Nutrition Planning

A 24-page guide to "Nutrition: Food at Work for You" (GS1), that's full of information about meal planning, buying and storing food, and the essential nutrients. Includes a daily food guide. Ask for by name and number.

**Send:** a postcard.
**To:** Publications Division, Office of Governmental and Public Affairs, U.S. Dept. of Agriculture, Washington, DC 20250

## Food Facts

A set of 5 illustrated pamphlets about food and nutrition, called the "Midget Encyclopedia." Each pamphlet deals with an issue of interest to consumers — food labels (and what's missing from them), cholesterol and disease, the food industry, additives, etc.

**Send:** $1.00.
**To:** Center for Science in the Public Interest, Dept. FS, 1755 S St., N.W., Washington, DC 20009

### TEENS AND ADULTS
- During their teens, boys and girls grow at a faster rate than at any other time except in infancy.
- Men and women 55 to 75 years old need 150 to 200 fewer calories per day than when they were 35 to 55, but their needs for essential nutrients are unchanged.

### VITAMIN A
- Vitamin A is needed for normal growth and for normal vision in dim light. It also helps keep the skin and inner linings of the body healthy and resistant to infection.
- Liver is outstanding for vitamin A. Important amounts are also found in eggs, butter, margarine, whole milk and cheese made with whole milk.

### STARCHES
Somehow, people got the idea that bread, potatoes and other starchy foods are fattening. We eat about half as much of these foods as we did in the early 1900s. We have replaced these starchy foods by foods that are high in fat and sugar. If anything is fattening, it is fat and sugar.

69

# NUTRITION INFORMATION

## Scorecard

A 32-page booklet, the "Food Scorecard," that helps parents and children assess the nutritional value of their meals. Discusses nutrition and food groups from the perspective of school children, rates various kinds of foods, and provides a "scorecard" to tally up a day's worth of meals.

**Send:** $1.00.
**To:** Center for Science in the Public Interest, Dept. FS, 1755 S St., N.W., Washington, DC 20009

### BREAKFAST FOODS

| (1 oz. portion) | % sugar |
|---|---|
| Quaker Oatmeal | 0 |
| Wheat Chex | 6 |
| Special K | 7 |
| Raisin Bran | 14 |
| Froot Loops | 49 |
| Sugar Smacks | 56 |

## Nutrient Density

A large 17x24-inch "Nutrient Density Chart" that illustrates the ratio of nutrients to calories in hundreds of foods, each of which is given a score. Includes complete information on how these scores are calculated and what they mean.

**Send:** $1.00.
**To:** The Basic & Traditional Food Assn., 1707 N St., N.W., Washington, DC 20036

### DEFINITION

Nutrient density is the ratio of nutrients to calories in a food. A food's nutrient content is divided by its calorie content to get a score for each nutrient. For example, if a food provides 10% of the protein allowance and 5% of the calorie allowance, it has a score of 2 for protein. The scores for 8 different nutrients are added to give the Nutrient Density Scores.

## Nutritive Values

A large 40-page guide to the "Nutritive Value of Foods" (G72). The bulk of it is a table of nutritive values for household measures of commonly used foods, from almonds to yogurt. Also includes a discussion of recommended Daily Allowances. Ask for by name and number.

**Send:** a postcard.
**To:** Publications Division, Office of Governmental and Public Affairs, U.S. Dept. of Agriculture, Washington, DC 20250

### RECOMMENDED DAILY DIETARY ALLOWANCES

**Females** (ages 23 to 50), (weight: 128 lbs.), (height: 65 inches) — 2000 calories, 46 grams of protein, 800 milligrams of calcium, 800 milligrams of phosphorous, 18 milligrams of iron, 1 milligram of thiamin, 1.2 milligrams of riboflavin, 13 milligrams of niacin, 45 milligrams of ascorbic acid, and 4000 international units of vitamin A.

## Food Labels

A large 57-page booklet, called "Nutrition Labeling — Tools For Its Use" (AB 382), that's designed to help people use the nutrition information on food labels to check and improve their diets. Includes a table showing the amounts of calories, proteins, vitamins and minerals supplied by 900 foods. Ask for by name and number.

**Send:** a postcard.
**To:** Publications Division, Office of Governmental and Public Affairs, U.S. Dept. of Agriculture, Washington, DC 20250

### BROCCOLI
1 medium-size stalk of broccoli, cooked, drained:
**Food Energy** — 45 calories
**Percentage of U.S. Recommended Daily Allowance** — Protein (8%), Vitamin A (90%), Vitamin C (270%), Thiamin (10%), Riboflavin (20%), Niacin (6%), Calcium (15%), and Iron (8%).

## Food Safety

A 12-page pamphlet, "Does Everything Cause Cancer?" that answers questions people ask most often about saccharin, nitrites, animal studies, and current food safety laws. Attempts to counter the arguments often used by the food industry.

**Send:** $1.00.
**To:** Center for Science in the Public Interest, Dept. FS, 1755 S St., N.W., Washington, D.C. 20009

### CARCINOGENS
**Q.** Is there a safe dose of a carcinogen?
**A.** No. Virtually all cancer experts agree that, in light of our limited knowledge of carcinogenesis, we must assume that if large doses of a chemical cause cancer, smaller doses also cause cancer, but less frequently.

## Food Additives

An 8-page booklet from the FDA that tells you "More Than You Ever Thought You Would Know About Food Additives." Discusses why additives are used and how they're regulated. Includes an index of over 130 additives.

**Send:** a postcard.
**To:** Consumer Information Center, Dept. 545 H, Pueblo, CO 81009

### DEFINITIONS
**Nutrients:** enrich (replace vitamins and minerals lost in processing) or fortify (add nutrients that may be lacking in the diet).
**Preservatives** (Antimicrobials): prevent food spoilage from bacteria, molds, fungi and yeast; extend shelf life; or protect natural color/flavor.

# NUTRITION INFORMATION

## High-Fiber Diets

A 2-page discussion of fiber, "Grandma Called It Roughage." Presents the claims and facts about high-fiber diets, discusses the effect of such diets on health, and lists some food sources of fiber.

**Send:** a postcard.
**To:** Consumer Information Center, Dept. 546 H, Pueblo, CO 81009

### SOURCES

For those who wish to increase their fiber intake, the FDA recommends eating more whole grain breads and cereals and fresh fruits and vegetables. But even dietary fiber that occurs naturally in food should be taken in moderation. Fiber advocates themselves warn against too sudden a change in the diet; it takes time for the digestive system to adapt.

## Dietary Minerals

A 4-page foldout from the FDA, called "A Primer on Dietary Minerals." Describes the minerals that are necessary for good health and growth, and lists the best food sources of these minerals.

**Send:** a postcard.
**To:** Consumer Information Center, Dept. 548 H, Pueblo, CO 81009

### MINERAL INTAKE

Taking too much of one essential mineral may upset the balance and function of other minerals in the body. Excess mineral intake can reduce an individual's ability to perform physical tasks and can contribute to such health problems as anemia, bone demineralization and breakage, neurological disease and fetal abnormalities.

## Fats

A short 10-page booklet that discusses "Fats in Food and Diet" (AB 361). Explains what fats are, lists the fat and cholesterol content of various foods, and outlines some theories about the role of fats in cardiovascular disease. Ask for by name and number.

**Send:** a postcard.
**To:** Publications Division, Office of Governmental and Public Affairs, U.S. Dept. of Agriculture, Washington, DC 20250

### CHOLESTEROL

Cholesterol is a normal constituent of blood and tissues and is found in every animal cell. Some of the cholesterol in human blood and tissues is synthesized by the body and some is supplied by diet. The amount supplied by diet varies greatly depending on the kinds and amounts of foods included.

## Citrus Fruits

A 4-page foldout full of "Questions and Answers about Vitamin C and Fresh Citrus Fruits" in which a nutritionist discusses what vitamin C is, how the body uses it, what foods provide it in significant amounts, and much more.

**Send:** a 9″ self-addressed, stamped envelope.
**To:** Consumer Services MP, Sunkist Growers, P.O. Box 7888, Van Nuys, CA 91409

## Raisins

"Raisin Nutrition," a short foldout that outlines the nutritional content of raisins. Discusses how much fiber, iron, potassium, calcium and protein raisins add to your diet, and explains that they are totally free of cholesterol and sucrose.

**Send:** a postcard.
**To:** California Raisin Advisory Board, P.O. Box 5335, Dept. FS, Fresno, CA 93755

### DAILY NEED

**Q.** I've heard that I need vitamin C every day. Why can't I eat a lot of foods with vitamin C one day and forget it for a while?

**A.** Vitamin C isn't stored in your body in any appreciable amount so you need a vitamin C-rich food every day. Because it is soluble in water, that which is not stored by the body is eliminated in the urine.

### FATS AND CARBOHYDRATES

- Raisins have only traces of fat and, of course, no cholesterol, a sterol found only in animal products.
- Raisins are 77 per cent carbohydrate primarily in the form of simple sugars — 45 per cent fructose and 55 per cent glucose. Raisins do not contain sucrose.

# NUTRITION INFORMATION

## Bean Nutrition

A small foldout that describes the nutritional value of all kinds of dry beans. "A Potful of Beans is a Pot Full of Nutrition" briefly discusses the amount of protein and the kinds of vitamins and minerals present in beans.

**Send:** a 9" self-addressed, stamped envelope.
**To:** California Dry Bean Advisory Board, P.O. Box 943, Dinuba, CA 93618

## Bread

A small 20-page booklet ("Bread on the Table") whose purpose is to explain in plain language the role that bread, and especially Roman Meal Bread, can play in a balanced nutrition program.

**Send:** a postcard.
**To:** Roman Meal Co., Consumer Services, Dept. M., 2101 S. Tacoma Way, Tacoma, WA 98409

## Health Foods

A 4-page foldout about "The Confusing World of Health Foods" that discusses the claims for "health," "organic" and "natural" foods. Compares the cost and nutritional value of health versus conventional foods.

**Send:** a postcard.
**To:** Consumer Information Center, Dept. 543 H, Pueblo, CO 81009

### FAT AND FIBER

- Beans contain no cholesterol unless animal fats are added in cooking or seasoning. Also, they are low in sodium. This is good news for persons on low cholesterol or low sodium diets.
- Beans do supply bulk and fiber for roughage, so important in regulating the digestion of our foods.

### MILLING

Ordinarily, the milling process breaks open the wheat kernel to extract the white flour. This rejects the wheat germ and the bran where most of the vitamins and minerals of the grain are located. However, the Roman Meal Company has a milling process that retains the germ and bran of both wheat and rye and adds additional bran and defatted flaxseed meal.

© Roman Meal Co.

### HERB TEAS

Herb teas, which are favored by many health food advocates, contain thousands of chemical compounds that have not been tested for safety. Sassafras root was found to contain safrole, which produces liver cancer in rats, and the sale of sassafras tea was banned by FDA in 1976 for that reason.

## Health & Diet

A 22-page booklet called "Your Diet: Health is in the Balance." Discusses what a balanced diet is and why it's important, how to watch and control caloric intake, and how to prepare a good meal plan.

**Send:** a postcard.
**To:** The Nutrition Foundation, Inc., Office of Education and Public Affairs, 888-17th St., N.W., Washington, DC 20006

## Overweight

A 14-page booklet, called "Overweight and Your Health . . . the Vital Connection," in which the medical director of Weight Watchers International discusses the relationship between obesity and respiratory problems, cardiovascular disease, and other medical hazards.

**Send:** a postcard.
**To:** Weight Watchers International, Inc., 800 Community Dr., Manhasset, NY 11030

## Weight Control

A 14-page booklet, called "Nutrition, Weight Control and You!" written by the medical director of Weight Watchers International. Discusses the essentials of good nutrition and outlines the nutritional aspects of the Weight Watchers program.

**Send:** a postcard.
**To:** Weight Watchers International, Inc., 800 Community Dr., Manhasset, NY 11030

### CALORIES

A calorie is a unit of measure, like a yardstick. For example, the length of an object is described in feet or inches. In precisely the same way, the energy value of a given food is expressed in calories. Similarly, the amount of energy expended in a particular body process or activity is also expressed in calories.

Reprinted with permission of The Nutrition Foundation.

### RESPIRATORY PROBLEMS

- Fat people tire more easily during physical exercise since muscle activity requires oxygen.
- Lack of oxygen and the resultant build-up of carbon dioxide in the body cause lethargy and sleepiness.

Reprinted with the permission of Weight Watchers International, Inc.

### BREAKFAST

Food intake should be distributed through the day, so that you take in food energy while expending physical energy. When you get up in the morning, you have not eaten for 6 to 8 hours. Roughly one-fourth of your total intake of food energy should be taken at breakfast.

Reprinted with the permission of Weight Watchers International, Inc.

# NUTRITION INFORMATION

## Snacks

A 14-page booklet that discusses "Snacking on a Weight-Control Program." Full of information about how to control the urge to eat snacks and how to snack wisely when you do eat between meals. Includes about a dozen recipes for low-calorie snacks.

**Send:** a postcard.
**To:** Weight Watchers International, Inc., 800 Community Dr., Manhasset, NY 11030

## Yogurt

A 45-page booklet, "Dieting, Yogurt and Common Sense," full of tips on how to diet sensibly, a calorie guide to common foods, and a set of menus that show you how to use yogurt in diets that limit your daily calories to 1000 or 1600.

**Send:** 25ᶜ.
**To:** Dorothy R. Young, Dannon Milk Products, Dept. FSC, 22-11 38th Ave., Long Island City, NY 11101

## Diet Plan

A long foldout that presents the "Roman Meal Diet Plan," listing full menus for 12 days, a calorie chart, an ideal weight chart, and a brief discussion of weight control. The diet is based on an average daily intake of 1200 calories.

**Send:** a postcard.
**To:** Roman Meal Co., Consumer Services, Dept. M, 2101 S. Tacoma Way, Tacoma, WA 98409

### Menu (Day 1)

Breakfast . . . . . . 195
- Orange Juice, ½ C
- Hard-cooked Egg, 1
- Roman Meal Toast, 1 sl.

Lunch . . . . . . 255
- Sandwich (tuna, 2 oz., tomato, 2 sl., lettuce, Roman Meal Bread, 2 sl.)
- Celery Sticks
- Apricots, 4 halves

Dinner . . . . . . 415
- Chicken Broth, 1 C
- Broiled Chicken Breast, 4 oz.
- Pineapple Rings, 2
- Steamed Asparagus, 6 spears
- Roman Meal Bread, 1 sl.
- Unsw. Baked Apple, 1 med. (before baking fill center with 1 T raisins)

Snacks . . . . . . 255
- Skim Milk, 2 C
- Carrot Sticks
- Cucumber Slices
- Low-cal Cottage Cheese, ⅓ C

TOTAL CALORIES FOR DAY . . . . . . . . . 1120

© Roman Meal Co.

## Lettuce Diet

A 10-page booklet, called "The California Iceberg Lettuce Primer," with advice on using low-calorie Iceberg lettuce (65-70 calories per 1½ lb. head) in your diet. Includes tips on buying, cleaning, storing lettuce, plus recipes for low-cal dressings and salads.

**Send:** a 9" self-addressed, stamped envelope.
**To:** California Iceberg Lettuce Commission, P.O. Box 3354, Monterey, CA 93940

## Pork Diet Plan

A short foldout, "Weight Watcher Primer on Pork," with recipes and advice for using pork, a food that is high in protein and can be purchased in lean cuts, on the Weight Watchers Food Plan. Recipes include Oriental Pork Chops and Roast Pork with Sage Sauce.

**Send:** a 9" self-addressed, stamped envelope.
**To:** Recipes, Missouri Pork Producers Assn., 922 Fourth St., #10D, Boonville, MO 65233

## 7-Day Diet

A colorful foldout, the "Romertopf Seven Day Diet," that describes how to cook meals in clay pots, which help food retain its essential nutrients and requires little or no fats or oils. Menus for a complete week are provided, and each day's calorie intake is identified.

**Send:** a 9" self-addressed, stamped envelope.
**To:** Margaret Meyer, Reco International Corp.—MP, P.O. Box 951, Port Washington, NY 11050

### Weightless Iceberg Wedges

1 head Iceberg lettuce
¼ C cold water
⅓ C instant non-fat dry milk
1½ C small curd cottage cheese
⅓ C crumbled Blue Cheese (1½ oz.)
3 T lemon juice
¾ t onion salt
¼ t garlic salt
2 tomatoes, sliced
Parsley

Core, rinse and thoroughly drain lettuce; chill in plastic bag. Combine remaining ingredients except parsley in electric blender; whir until blended and fairly smooth. Cover and chill. Cut lettuce into 6 narrow wedges; arrange with tomato on chilled salad plates and spoon dressing atop. Garnish with minced parsley. Makes 6 servings.

# NUTRITION INFORMATION

## Meat & Diets

A large foldout, called "Dietary Fitness: A Meat Lover's Guide," that discusses the role meat plays in diets. Includes a number of features — a protein density chart, fat and cholesterol content charts, calorie charts. Another chart compares the nutritive value of Oscar Mayer's products with that of other foods.

**Send:** a postcard.
**To:** Consumer Affairs Dept., Oscar Mayer and Co., P.O. Box 7188—FSFC, Madison, WI 53707

## Low-Cal Protein Diets

A 4-page foldout from the FDA about "Low-Calorie Protein Diets." Explores the safety questions about using low-calorie protein products to lose weight, and explains FDA labeling requirements.

**Send:** a postcard.
**To:** Consumer Information Center, Dept. 542 H, Pueblo, CO 81009

## Rice & Diets

A recipe foldout, called "Calculated Cooking," with a variety of rice recipes for those on a diabetic or modified exchange diet. Each of the 14 recipes also lists the caloric content of each serving and the exchange value of the ingredients.

**Send:** a postcard.
**To:** Rice Council of America, Dept. FM, P.O. Box 22802, Houston, TX 77027

### Spinach Au Gratin

Each Serving Provides:
172 calories
½ meat exchange
1 bread exchange
½ fat exchange
½ vegetable exchange

**2 pkgs. (10 oz. each) frozen chopped spinach**
**3 C cooked rice**

**4 eggs, beaten**
**1 can (10¾ oz.) condensed cream of mushroom soup**
**Dash of nutmeg**
**1 t onion powder**
**½ t salt**
**¼ t pepper**
**¼ C grated Parmesan cheese**

Thaw, drain and separate spinach. Toss with rice. Combine eggs, soup and seasonings. Stir into spinach mixture. Turn into a greased shallow 2½-quart casserole. Sprinkle top with Parmesan cheese. Bake at 350° for 30 minutes or until firm. Makes 8 servings.

# CATALOGS

# CATALOGS

**Note:** the HIGHLIGHTS listed on each page of this section represent the kinds of cookware, foods and books that can be ordered from the catalogs described there. However, these items are **not free;** they can only be ordered from the catalogs themselves, not from Free Stuff for Cooks.

## Cross Imports

A 68-page, fully illustrated "Shop by Mail and Recipe Book" that lists over 700 gourmet gadgets, knives and cookware available through the mail. The catalog also includes 50 recipes and a selection of discount coupons.

**Send:** $1.00.
**To:** Cross Imports, Inc., 210—MP Hanover St., Boston, MA 02113

### HIGHLIGHTS

- The new Italian CROSS Noodle Machine
- Fish Poacher — brightly tinned heavy steel with a pullup rack
- Dough Scraper — 1-piece stainless steel, both the blade and the handle
- Le Creuset skillets, sauce pans, round pots

## Figi's

"The Cook's Collection," a copy of Figi's colorful mail order catalog. Includes various kinds of glassware, porcelain, metal cookware (including copper), knives, bowls, utensils and appliances, and imported and specialty foods.

**Send:** a postcard.
**To:** Figi's, Inc., Marshfield, WI 54449

## Williams-Sonoma

Williams-Sonoma's colorful 50-page "Catalog for Cooks," that lists all sorts of things that cooks will be interested in getting through the mail. Includes gourmet cookware, utensils, food processors, convection ovens, pasta makers and gourmet foods.

**Send:** a postcard.
**To:** Williams-Sonoma, Mail Order Dept. 6558, P.O. Box 3792, San Francisco, CA 94119

### HIGHLIGHTS

- Calaphon casseroles, stock pots, sauce pans, omelet pans
- The Sama Machine, an Italian expresso and cappuccino maker
- English Blue Band Earthenware Bowls

# CATALOGS

## Lillian Vernon

Lillian Vernon's large, colorful "Country Gourmet" catalog that features all sorts of fine gourmet gifts, serving accessories, kitchen work and space savers available through the mail.

**Send:** 25ᶜ.
**To:** Lillian Vernon's Country Gourmet, Box LV, Dept. FXSC, 510 S. Fulton Ave., Mt. Vernon, NY 10551

### HIGHLIGHTS
- Cast aluminum stock pot — 6-quart size, 8″ across, 7″ deep
- Stemware rack — hangs up to 16 glasses upside down
- Earthenware casseroles — set of 2, each holds 16 oz.
- White porcelain mortar and pestle set

## Colonial Garden Kitchens

"A Treasury of Gourmet Cookware, Gadgets & Gifts," Colonial Garden Kitchens' catalog, featuring over 1000 foods, cookware, and kitchen gadgets available through the mail. Includes everything from egg coddlers to Queen Anne casseroles.

**Send:** 25ᶜ.
**To:** Colonial Garden Kitchens, Dept. FSOC, 270 W. Merrick Rd., Valley Stream, NY 11582

## Green Mountain Sugar House

A 16-page catalog that will introduce you to the world of Vermont maple syrup. Includes a discussion of how syrup is made and what its various grades are. Lists various syrups, jams, jellies, cheeses and meats available through the mail.

**Send:** a postcard.
**To:** Green Mountain Sugar House, Dept. FSC, RFD 1, Ludlow, VT 05149

### HIGHLIGHTS
- Vermont Maple Syrup, by the gallon, the quart or the pint
- Vermont Breakfast Package — 1 quart of Vermont Grade A Maple Syrup, 1 lb. of Vermont Corn-Cob Smoked Bacon, and a 2-lb. package of Buckwheat Pancake Mix
- Vermont Cheddar Cheese, in 3-lb. and 5-lb. wheels

## Hegg & Hegg

The "Gourmet Gift Harvest from the Pacific Northwest," a short foldout that describes various gift packs featuring salmon, tuna, sturgeon, clams and shrimp that are available through the mail from Hegg & Hegg.

**Send:** a postcard.
**To:** Hegg & Hegg Smoked Salmon, Inc., 802 Marine Dr., Port Angeles, WA 98362

## Chrisman Farms

A colorful mail order catalog from Chrisman Farms that lists various meats, cheeses, fruitcakes, syrups, dressings and sauces that are available. Also includes a couple of information sheets about using their products and a $2.00 discount coupon.

**Send:** $1.00.
**To:** Chrisman Farms, P.O. Box 79, Mapleton, IA 51034

## Harrington's

A copy of Harrington's current mail order catalog, which lists smoked hams, bacon, sausage, smoked turkey and pheasant, cheeses, maple syrups, and many other products, including various gift packs and samples. Complete instructions for ordering.

**Send:** a postcard.
**To:** Harrington's, 2B11-O Main St., Richmond, VT 05477

### HIGHLIGHTS
- Smoked Seafood Sampler — quarter pound tins of Smoked Salmon, Smoked Oysters, Smoked Sturgeon and Smoked Clams
- De Luxe Party Pack Basket — a variety of tinned seafood, all packed in a large willow tray

### HIGHLIGHTS
- Smokehouse Sample Box — ½ Ham, 1 lb. Sliced Bacon, 1½ lbs. Canadian Bacon
- Smoked Irish Salmon
- Cheese Sampler — ½ lb. Cheddar, ½ lb. Vermont Blue Cheese, ½ lb. Hickory & Maple Smoked Cheese, ½ lb. Green Mountain Jack and ½ lb. Smoked Cheese with Sausage

# CATALOGS

## Aunt Lucy Hams

A full-color mail order brochure that lists the various "Country Foods" available from Aunt Lucy Hams. Products include ham, bacon, smoked sausage, smoked turkey, and canned goods like pudding, corn meal and flour.

**Send:** 25¢.
**To:** Aunt Lucy Hams, Inc., P.O. Box 126, Dept. CFB, Walkersville, MD 21793

### HIGHLIGHTS

- One-year-old or six-month-old Hams
- Hickory Smoked Sausage and whole Smoked Turkeys
- Canned products — Crumbly Sausage, Scrapple and Country Puddin'
- Old-fashioned Yellow or White Corn Meal

## Omaha Steaks

A full-color gourmet foods catalog called "Elegant Moments" that shows a variety of top quality steaks, gourmet meats and heat-and-serve entrees you can order by mail. A $5.00 discount certificate that can be used with your first order is included.

**Send:** $1.00.
**To:** Omaha Steaks International, Dept. 3437, 4400 S. 96th St., Omaha, NE 68127

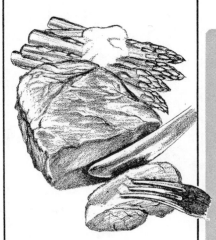

## Swiss Cheese Shop

A colorful mail order brochure from The Swiss Cheese Shop that describes a variety of bulk crock and gift pack cheeses available, including cheddars, wine cheese, hot pepper cheese, muenster and more.

**Send:** a postcard.
**To:** The Swiss Cheese Shop, P.O. Box 429, Dept. SFC, Monroe, WI 53566

### HIGHLIGHTS

- Cheese Crock Trio — 3 crocks of Sharp Cheddar, Smoked Cheddar and Wine Cheddar Spreads
- Cheese 'n Sausage — Summer Sausage Links, plus Swiss Sharp Cheddar, Caraway and Colby Cheeses
- Cholest Free — a cholesterol-free cheese imported from Sweden.

## Paprikas Weiss

A copy of Paprikas Weiss's current "Imported Foods and Cookware Catalogue," from the company that specializes in Hungarian imports. Features herbs and spices (including its famous paprikas), candies, pastries, meats, cheeses, enamel cookware and more.

**Send:** a postcard.
**To:** Paprikas Weiss, Dept. FSFC, 1546 Second Ave., New York, NY 10028

### HIGHLIGHTS
- Sweet, Half-Sweet, or Hot Paprika (in 1-lb., 5-lb., and 10-lb. containers)
- Romanian Salami
- Irish Beef Steak & Kidney Pie
- Hungarian-Style Dumplings
- Austrian Triple-Coated Enamel Cookware

## Bissinger's

"The Gourmet's Catalogue," Bissinger's directory of chocolates, candies, fruit bars, cookies, nuts and other gourmet goods available by mail. Various assortments and gift packs available.

**Send:** 25¢.
**To:** Bissinger's, Dept. FS, 205 W. Fourth St., Cincinnati, OH 45202

## China Bowl Trading

A colorful catalog sheet, price list, and order form that features the imported noodles, oils, flavorings, herbs, spices, dried mushrooms and other specialties that are available from the China Bowl Trading Company.

**Send:** a 9" self-addressed, stamped envelope.
**To:** China Bowl Trading Co., Inc., 80 Fifth Ave., New York, NY 10011

### HIGHLIGHTS
- Light and Dark Soy Sauce (in 5- and 12-oz. bottles)
- Hosein Sauce (in a 6-oz. jar)
- Szechuan Peppercorns (in a 1-oz. jar)
- Black Mushrooms and Sliced Mushrooms (in 1-oz. boxes)
- Cellophane Noodles

# CATALOGS

## Penn Herb

A large 58-page catalog from the Penn Herb Co. that lists over 400 herbs and spices, herb seeds and related herbal products available through the mail. Also includes a lot of information about herbs and their use.

**Send:** a postcard.
**To:** Penn Herb Co., Ltd., Dept. 101, 603 N. 2nd St., Philadelphia, PA 19123

## Grace Tea

A 4-page brochure and mail order form from the Grace Rare Tea Co. that describes the various black and oolong teas that this company imports and makes available in attractive canisters. Also includes tips on how to make a good cup of tea.

**Send:** a 9″ self-addressed, stamped envelope.
**To:** Grace Tea Co., Ltd., 80 Fifth Ave., New York, NY 10011

## W. T. Rawleigh

A colorful shopping guide to the W. T. Rawleigh Company's products, which include seasonings, syrups, soup and salad mixes, and desserts. Other household products (shampoos, cleansers, vitamin supplements) are also described.

**Send:** 25ᶜ.
**To:** W. T. Rawleigh Company, 223 E. Main St., Freeport, IL 61032

### HIGHLIGHTS

Star Anise, Sweet Basil Herb, Bay Leaves, Bitter Orange Peel, Cayenne Pepper, Chicory Root, Cinnamon Sticks, Coriander Seed, Fennel Seed, Hops, Jasmine, Papaya-Mint Tea, Red Sage, Sweet Marjoram, Vanilla Beans

### HIGHLIGHTS

- Salad Dressing Mixes (Green Onion & Garlic, Thousand Island, Italian, Blue Cheese, French)
- Seasonings and Spices (Barbecue Spice, Chicken Seasoning, Hickory Smoke Salt and many more)
- Create a Soup! Instant Soup Base (Chicken or Beef)

## Woodbridge Press

A copy of Woodbridge Press's current catalog of books, which lists a wide variety of books on health, nutrition and cooking, including titles like *The Mushroom Growing & Cooking Book, How to Survive Snack Attacks—Naturally,* and *The Art of Home Cheesemaking.*

**Send:** 25¢.
**To:** Woodbridge Press Publishing Co., P.O. Box 6189, Santa Barbara, CA 93111

### HIGHLIGHTS
* *Natural Sweets and Treats,* by Ruth Laughlin. More than 300 ways to prepare sweets and treats from natural, wholesome ingredients.
* *Dry and Save,* by Dora D. Flack. Practical guidebook for home food drying, with recipes for using dehydrated foods.

## Presque Isle Wine Cellars

"Everything for the Home Winemaker," a catalog that delivers on what its title promises. Includes a checklist of equipment for beginning winemakers, plus descriptions of all sorts of books, chemicals, bottles, wine presses and other equipment available through the mail from Presque Isle.

**Send:** a postcard.
**To:** Presque Isle Wine Cellars, 9440 Buffalo Rd., North East, PA 16428

## Aurora Book Companions

A copy of "Health-Related Books," a large catalog that lists over 2000 books available through the mail from one source. Includes general health books as well as cookbooks for special types of diets. Books are listed by title and cross-referenced by category.

**Send:** 15¢.
**To:** Aurora Book Companions, Dept. FSC, P.O. Box 5852, Denver, CO 80217

### HIGHLIGHTS
* *Salt-Free Diet Cookbook* (Conason, M.D.)
* *Why Your Child Is Hyperactive* (Feingold)
* *Nutrition Almanac* (Kirschmann)
* *Sprouts — How to Grow & Eat Them* (Allen)
* *Vegetarian Cookery* (Walker)

# CATALOGS

## Consumer Catalog

A copy of the current "Consumer Information Catalog," which lists hundreds of free or inexpensive pamphlets and booklets available from almost 30 agencies of the Federal government. Many of the publications deal with food, cooking, nutrition and health.

**Send:** a postcard.
**To:** Current Catalog, Consumer Information Center, Pueblo, CO 81009

### HIGHLIGHTS
- *Safe Brown Bag Lunches.* Types of food best suited for packed lunches; precautions to assure wholesomeness.
- *Your Money's Worth in Foods.* Guides for budgeting, meal planning, and shopping for best values.

## Government Publications

Four catalogs of documents that are sold by the U.S. Government Printing Office. These catalogs list and describe various pamphlets and booklets made available on the subject of food, cooking and nutrition. Ask for each catalog that you want by name and number.

**Canning, Freezing and Storage of Foods (SB005)**
**Cookbooks and Recipes (SB065)**
**Home Economics (SB276)**
**Food, Diet and Nutrition (SB291)**

**Send:** a postcard.
**To:** Superintendent of Documents, U.S. Government Printing Office, Washington, DC 20402

### HIGHLIGHTS
- *Baking for People with Food Allergies.* A booklet of special recipes that eliminate wheat, eggs or milk from the diets of people who are allergic to one or more of these foods.
- *Fish and Shellfish over the Coals.* More than 35 recipes for tasty seafood delicacies and delicious seafood dinners are the feature in this booklet.
- *USDA Grade Standards for Food, How They Are Developed and Used.* Provides a brief summary of the origin and purpose of the USDA grading program, outlines the manner in which the standards are developed, and discusses the techniques and operations of the program.

## Culinary Arts

A sample copy of *The Charity Cookbook Collector,* a catalog of charity and community cookbooks — recipes collected by groups of people to benefit a charity. Over 80 cookbooks are described and information about ordering books through the mail is provided.

**Send:** $1.00.
**To:** Culinary Arts Catalogue Co., 223 Prince St., P.O. Box 369 MP, Tappahannock, VA 22560

### HIGHLIGHTS
- *Recipes and Reminiscences of New Orleans.* 400 recipes, some contributed by famous restaurants in the city, collected by the Old Ursuline Convent Guild.
- *Recipes from Old Virginia.* 700 old and new Virginia recipes, collected by the Virginia Extension Homemakers Council.

## Sunset Books

A copy of the current "Sunset Books Catalog," a colorful foldout that describes dozens of books and shows you how to get them by mail. Among their almost 2 dozen cookbooks are books about wok, microwave and food processor cookery.

**Send:** a 9″ self-addressed, stamped envelope.
**To:** Sunset Books Mail Order—FS, Lane Publishing Company, Willow & Middlefield Rds., Menlo Park, CA 94025

## 101 Productions

101 Productions' catalog of books, which includes an attractive assortment of diet, ethnic, and general cookbooks. Plus a packet of 6 cards, each with a recipe excerpted from one of 101's books.

**Send:** 25¢.
**To:** 101 Productions, Dept. FS, 834 Mission St., San Francisco, CA 94103

### HIGHLIGHTS
- *International Fish Cookery,* by Lou Seibert. A collection of 200 fish recipes from 2 dozen countries.
- *The Calculating Cook,* by Jeanne Jones. A gourmet cookbook for diabetics and dieters.
- *Middle Eastern Cookery,* by Eva Zane. 165 recipes from Persia, Turkey, Armenia, Syria, Lebanon, Israel and North Africa.

# CATALOGS

## Garden Way

Garden Way's catalog of publications, which lists a complete selection of cookbooks and bulletins (including *Mushroom Cookery, Woodstove Cookery, The Sprouter's Cookbook* ) and other books on cooking, canning and preserving. Also lists books for gardeners and homeowners.

**Send:** 25¢ plus a 9″ self-addressed, stamped envelope.
**To:** Garden Way Publishing, Dept. A 268B, Charlotte, VT 05445

### HIGHLIGHTS
- *Zucchini Cookbook,* by Nancy Ralston and Marynor Jordan. Over 250 recipes for appetizers, casseroles, desserts, salads, stews and more.
- *Treasured Recipes from Early New England Kitchens,* by Marjorie Blanchard. 133 classic specialties all updated for today's kitchen.

## Nilgiri Press

A mail-order flyer that will introduce you to *Laurel's Kitchen,* a popular vegetarian cookbook and handbook on nutrition. The large flyer reprints a few of the book's pages and provides examples of the attractive woodcuts that illustrate the book.

**Send:** a postcard.
**To:** *Laurel's Kitchen* Flyer, Nilgiri Press, P.O. Box 477, Petaluma, CA 94952

Welcome to Laurel's Kitchen

## Cookbook Club

A short leaflet that describes The Cookery Book Club, a club that offers cookbooks at discount rates to members. (Membership costs $5.00.) Leaflet lists some of the books available through the club.

**Send:** a postcard.
**To:** The Cookery Book Club, P.O. Box 768, Port Washington, NY 11050

### HIGHLIGHTS
- *A History of Gastronomy,* by Jay Jacobs. The evolution of the world's greatest cuisines.
- *German Home Baking,* by Dr. August Oetker. Original creations and traditional favorites.

# POSTERS
# SAMPLES AND
# NEWSLETTERS

# POSTERS SAMPLES & NEWSLETTERS

## Posters

A set of 2 approximately 10x14-inch posters, which are antiqued parchment replicas of actual historical documents. The posters, called "Fare of Ye Tavern" and "Rules of This Tavern," list old menus and can be framed and used as kitchen decorations.

**Send:** $1.00.
**To:** Historical Documents Co., Dept. C110, 8 N. Preston, Philadelphia, Pa 19104

## Sample Spices

Sample packets of 3 of Gayelord Hauser's special seasoners — Vege-Sal, Spike, and Vegit. Each seasoner is a blend of natural ingredients and can be used in soups, salads, main dishes — anywhere that salt can be used.

**Send:** a 9″ self-addressed, stamped envelope.
**To:** Gayelord Hauser Recommended Products, P.O. Box 09398, Dept. FS, Milwaukee, WI 53209

## Herbs & Seeds

A collection of 8 seed packets, including basil, caraway, chives, chervil, dill, savory, sorrel and roquette, to help you start your own herb garden. Also includes planting instructions and some recipes for using herbs in salads, dressings, soups and main dishes.

**Send:** $1.00.
**To:** Le Jardin Du Gourmet, P.O. Box 146, West Danville, VT 05873

## Measuring Spoon

A handy stainless steel measuring gauge, called the "1 Equals 7 Spoon" because it adjusts quickly to 7 different positions (from ¼ teaspoon to 1 tablespoon). A precision spoon that any cook will find useful.

**Send:** 75°.
**To:** The Pine Cone, Dept. MP—81, Blake Bldg., Gilroy, CA 95020

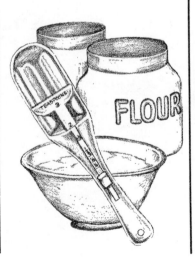

## Popcorn Ball Maker

A bright red plastic popcorn ball maker that will allow you to make popcorn balls without burning your fingers or getting them all sticky. Includes instructions and a recipe.

**Send:** $1.00.
**To:** Jolly Time Pop Corn, American Pop Corn Co., P.O. Box 178, Dept. M, Sioux City, IA 51102

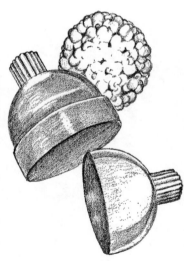

## Wine

A sample copy of a weekly newspaper, *The Wine Spectator,* that covers the American wine industry. Each issue contains news stories, book reviews, editorials, recipes, columns, a list of wine tastings and seminars, and a business directory of wineries, wine publications, distributors and retailers.

**Send:** $1.00.
**To:** The Wine Spectator, 4017 Brant St., San Diego, CA 92103

## Microwaves

A sample copy of *Microgram,* a bi-monthly newsletter "dedicated to the art of microwave cookery." Each issue includes cooking tips, at least a dozen recipes, and information about books and booklets of interest to microwave users.

**Send:** $1.00.
**To:** Microwave Resources, P.O. Box 2301—FS, Pasco, WA 99302

## Clay Cooking

A sample copy of *Cooking in Clay,* a 4-page newsletter devoted to Romertopf Clay Pot Cookery. Issues regularly feature cooking tips, recipes, information about nutrition and diet, and news about related products and cookbooks.

**Send:** a 9" self-addressed, stamped envelope.
**To:** Margaret Meyer, Reco International Corp.—MP, P.O. Box 951, Port Washington, NY 11050

## Refunding

A sample copy of *The Refundle Bundle,* a monthly newsletter that tells you all about "cashing in at the checkout." Each issue is packed with information about refunds, coupons, offers, freebies. Includes tips and advice on how to take advantage of these offers and save money at the grocery store.

**Send:** $1.00.
**To:** Refundle Bundle, P.O. Box 141, Dept. FSFC, Centuck Station, Yonkers, NY 10710

# NEWSLETTERS

## Food & Health

A sample copy of *Nutrition Action,* a monthly newsletter that regularly features stories on the food industry, reports on the latest health and nutrition research, letters from readers, editorials, book reviews and resource lists. Written for consumers.

**Send:** $1.00.
**To:** Center for Science in the Public Interest, Dept. FS, 1755 S St., N.W., Washington, DC 20009

## Nutrition

A sample copy of a newsletter called *Nutrition News,* prepared by the Roman Meal Company. Each issue discusses some subject of current interest, like food fiber, physical fitness, nutrition and alcohol. Also includes some useful tips on nutrition as well as a recipe intended to stretch the food value of your dollars.

**Send:** a postcard.
**To:** Roman Meal Co., Consumer Services, Dept. M, 2101 S. Tacoma Way, Tacoma, WA 98409

## Kids & Nutrition

A sample copy of *Practical Parenting,* Vicki Lansky's helpful hints newsletter. Each issue offers recipes; practical advice from parents about feeding kids; nutrition information; consumer tips; food news items; and lots of other information about parenting.

**Send:** $1.00.
**To:** Practical Parenting, P.O. Box 638, Wayzata, MN 55391

# INDEX

# INDEX

# INDEX

# MORE FROM MEADOWBROOK PRESS...

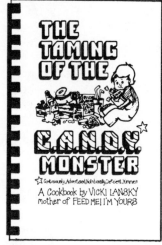

Meadowbrook Press
Wayzata, MN 55391

OVER 250 FUN
THINGS INSIDE

2⁹⁵

**The best of free and up-to-a-dollar
things kids can send for by mail!**

**FEED ME! I'M YOURS**
**By Vicki Lansky**

America's #1 cookbook for new mothers.
Tells how to make baby food at home
plus delicious, nutritious alternatives to
junk food for pre-schoolers. Over 200
child-tested recipes. Spiral bound.

**TAMING THE C.A.N.D.Y. MONSTER**
**By Vicki Lansky**

#1 New York Times Best-Seller! Tells
how to get your children to eat less
sugar and salt. Over 200 recipes and
ideas for better snacks, desserts,
brown-bag lunches, traveling meals.

**FREE STUFF FOR KIDS**
**By The Free Stuff Editors**

The best of free and up-to-a-dollar things kids can send for by
mail. Includes offers of posters, coins, pamphlets, decals, crafts,
games and more.

**THESE BOOKS ARE AVAILABLE AT YOUR
BOOK STORE OR GIFT STORE, OR BY MAIL.**